IN SEARCH OF YOUR GERMAN ROOTS

Angus Baxter

In Search of Your German Roots

**A COMPLETE GUIDE TO TRACING
YOUR ANCESTORS IN THE
GERMANIC AREAS OF EUROPE**

Third Edition

**GENEALOGICAL
PUBLISHING CO., INC.**

First Edition 1987
Second Edition ("United Germany Edition") 1991
Third Edition 1994
Second printing of the Third Edition 1995
Third printing of the Third Edition 1996

Published by Genealogical Publishing Co., Inc.
1001 N. Calvert Street, Baltimore, MD 21202
Library of Congress Catalogue Card Number 94-76790
International Standard Book Number 0-8063-1447-8
Made in the United States of America

Cover photograph by Michael Philip Manheim, courtesy of Folio, Inc.

FOR NAN—my love, my life, my wife

I have not sung for you
One line of all the tribute I would pay
Yet, oh, if you knew
The things that crowd in my head
At the thought of you
Then would you say
"To me belongs
The Song of Songs."

(a poem by Cecil Roberts)

CONTENTS

INTRODUCTION

This book is written to help you trace your ancestors in the "old country"—whether your German forebears came from Germany or Austria or one of the many European countries that had German settlements. It will give you very little information about records on this side of the Atlantic because there are many books available on this subject. Of course, I will talk about major areas of German settlement in North America, such as Pennsylvania and the Midwest, and the Kitchener area of Canada.

Why should you bother to trace your ancestors—those unknown men and women who created you? What benefits will you obtain from your search?

There are no easy answers to these questions but your place in the scheme of things will be more secure. You will know more about yourself and the members of your family who preceded you. When you start to search for your German ancestors you will be setting out on a journey of the heart and mind that will bring you happiness and romance beyond all measure.

No one can say for sure why, all over the world, men and women are searching for their roots. Some, perhaps, hope to find a missing family fortune, some a title of nobility held in abeyance until a claimant comes along, some want to impress their friends with the social standing of great-grandfather, or some to find a family coat of arms. However, I believe the answer is quite a simple one—we, or our children, simply want to know where our family originated and what our ancestors were like.

We want to know what they did, how they earned a living. Why did they leave home to cross the Atlantic? What was happening in their country at that moment in history? What clothes did they wear? What food did they eat? These are our questions and we are the people who will answer them if we are patient and determined.

As you travel back through the years you will acquire no financial

rewards—most family stories of missing fortunes are without any foun-
dation—but, on the other hand, you will not have to spend a great deal
of money. Of course, you can pay professional researchers to do your
work for you, but this is totally unnecessary. Genealogy is a do-it-
yourself hobby and this book is designed to help you do just that. Researchers will probably bring you results, but however good they are,
they will lack your great personal advantage—your love of your family.

You will need other assets, of course—an organized mind and the
patience and determination I mentioned above. You will meet with many
obstacles and frustrations. You will meet with difficulties and dead
ends. No one ever said ancestor-hunting was easy—or if they did, they
didn't know what they were talking about!

You will need to know your history, because the great and remarkable race from which you are so proudly descended has spread across
the continent of Europe. Great events of history have changed frontiers,
created new countries, destroyed old ones, and through all these cata-
clysms the German race has left its mark in many areas far beyond the
borders of what we now call Germany.

Because you have a German surname and a family story that "great-
grandfather came from Germany," do not assume that he came from
that area of Europe marked "Germany" on the map. He could have
come from Austria, Belgium, the former Czechoslovakia, Denmark,
France, Italy, Liechtenstein, Poland, Romania, Switzerland, the former
USSR (including the Baltic states of Estonia, Latvia, and Lithuania), or
Yugoslavia. All these countries are either German-speaking or have
large German minorities. Do not be discouraged. The Germans in these
countries kept their own customs, their religion, their ancestral pride,
and their records. Their passion for order is a priceless legacy for you.

You can do all your searching by correspondence, by working in your
own home at your own pace, by using the resources of libraries and
archives or church and government records. You do not need to visit the
place from which your family came to this country—although one day
your own natural curiosity may take you there. Resist the temptation to
board a plane tomorrow. You will accomplish much more by sitting
down and reading this book—keeping it beside you as you search.

As your work progresses you will be corresponding with people in
the old country—priests and ministers, archivists and librarians, friendly
civil servants (yes, they do exist!), and genealogical and historical organizations. You will be making contacts and friends—and even distant
cousins who will welcome you when you do go overseas. By then, too,
you will have learned a great deal about your forebears; you will be able
to walk the fields they plowed, worship in the churches they attended,

visit the houses in which they lived, and you will not be a stranger in a strange land.

As you turn the pages of this book you will learn about the history of the German people; you will find out how to record the knowledge you will acquire; and you will find out the exact locations of sources of information.

How much will it all cost? How far back will you get? No one can tell you this—it will depend on you and on the state of the records in the area from which your family came. Remember that ancestor-hunting is a pay-as-you-go hobby, and your costs will be spread over a period of time. You, and only you, will control the expenditure. You and only you will decide if you should stop for a while (if you can!) and then start again. Never let this wonderful journey become a drain on your finances.

Don't take on too much research at a time. Start with just one side of your family, otherwise you will only become confused with the dozens of names you will collect as time goes by. "Was that Ernst Müller or Ernst Brand? Was it Anna Frank who came from Munich (München), or was that Anna Fiedler?" You will also find that when you are searching long lists of names it will be much easier to look for one surname than seven or eight. Of course, if two or more sides of your family came from the same village, that is quite a different story—you will save time and money by looking for them simultaneously.

With the passage of time your family tree will grow, and as it does you will find out many things about the people who made you. You will find answers to questions you have often asked, and to questions you have never known you wanted to ask. You may even discover physical appearances and traits of character that will tell you why you are as you are.

As you will read later on in this book, write to local newspapers in the old country and ask for information about your family—provided that you know the general area of the country from which they came. Your letter will probably be published if you keep it very short—or it may not. It may bring a response from a sixth cousin—or it may not. You do not know, but in ancestor-hunting you try every possible way to delve into the past. For example, you may be descended from those Germans who settled in Transylvania (then part of Hungary, now in Romania) in the twelfth century. There are still a sufficient number of Germans living in Romania to justify the publication of a weekly newspaper in German. You could try a letter to the editor of *Neuer Weg*, Piata Scinteii 1, Bucharest (Bucuresti), Romania. Who knows what results it will bring?

Finally, you must be warned that in your search, as you go further back in the records, you will be confronted with the old Germanic script. In its printed form it is not too difficult to grasp because it resembles the script used on the title page of many newspapers—the *New York Times*, for example. It is in its handwritten form that the real problems arise. A further complication is that the earlier church records were often written in Latin. I suggest you buy, or try and borrow through your library, an inexpensive booklet, *Decipher Germanic Records,* by Edna M. Bentz. It was privately published in San Diego in 1982. It is the most helpful book I know because it not only explains and illustrates Germanic script, but also lists handwritten examples of many of the words you will encounter in your own research—emigrant, sponsor, sergeant, innkeeper, lessee, miner, farmer, priest, settler, and so on.

Enough of these preliminary words of wisdom! With the aid of this book you are starting on an exciting voyage, and no one knows where it will take you or what treasures you will find along the way. Perhaps there really was a castle on the Rhine once owned by your family—maybe an ancestor stood on the battlements of Marksburg and watched the ships sail slowly by on the river far below. All this lies ahead with the discoveries you will make as you search for your German roots.

One last thing. This is an updated edition of a work that was originally published in 1985, and it therefore includes details of changes brought about by the re-unification of Germany into one single great nation. There will, doubtless, be more changes in the future. However, you will find here information about new addresses and names of places, and new locations of various archives, civil and ecclesiastical. So far as that area once known as "East Germany" is concerned, you will also discover changes in an attitude of mind when you make contact with authorities there—something that cannot be described in these pages!

Germany is now the second largest country in Europe, second only to Russia. The total population is over seventy-nine and a half million. Berlin is the official capital, but for the time being the government will remain in Bonn. The target date for removal from Bonn to Berlin is now 2000.

STARTING THE SEARCH

Start with you and with no one else. Do not take someone with your surname who was famous two centuries ago and try and trace his or her descendants down to you. First, it is impossible and, second, there is little likelihood of a family connection anyway. Names can be misleading in four ways:

1. Even within a few generations of a family the spelling of a name can change. Usually this was because, with a few exceptions, our ancestors could not read and write and so the name would be spelled phonetically (as it sounded). There was, in fact, a double complication, for the name could sound differently to different people. Just as some people are tone-deaf to music, so other people are word-deaf. The spelling changes could occur on different occasions—when your ancestor was arranging with the local clergyman for a baptism, a marriage, or a burial; when he was registering with the local police for an internal passport; when he was answering the questions of the census enumerator; when he was registering for compulsory military service; when he was booking passage on a ship; or even when a name was being carved on a tombstone. In my own family records you will find Baxter, Backster, Bagster, Bacaster, Bacster, Bakster, Bacchuster—even Bastar (I didn't like that one very much!). In Germany, for example, Meyer can be spelled as Mayer, Meier, Meir, Mier, or Maier.

2. Don't assume that everyone with the same name as yours must be related to you somewhere back in time. Up until the fourteenth century (and much later in some parts of Europe) there were no surnames. People were known by their first name, and attached to it was a word describing where they lived or what they did, or even an event such as a flood that took place when they were born. So a man named Wilhelm might be Wilhelm from the wood (Wald), or Wilhelm the baker (Bäcker), or Wilhelm the wagonmaker (Wagner), or Wilhelm born in the storm (Sturm). Sometimes, too, a newcomer to a village would be known, for

example, as Wilhelm from Erlangen (this would be written as Wilhelm von Erlangen, so I am sorry to say a "von" in your ancestral name does not necessarily mean your forebears were noblemen!). By about 1400 the population growth and increasing movement of the population made the lack of a surname a nuisance and so the "the" or "of" or "from" was dropped.

3. You may find your surname was changed a couple of generations back. This could happen for several reasons—your ancestor may have decided his name was too long or too complicated for use in a new country and so he might make it shorter; or he may have decided to anglicize his name so that Schmidt became Smith; or he might have encountered some bigot of an immigration officer who said, "Rosenkrantz? What sort of name is that? I'll put you down as Rose."

4. In certain areas, particularly in Holstein and Ostfriesland, the system of patronymics was used (giving children a surname based on their father's first name), so that Peter Bergmann could have a son with the name of Wilhelm Peters. In some cases, too, a man might have a surname based on the name of his farm, and if he moved to another farm his surname would change. However, patronymics and farm names are not always a problem because usually the real family name was entered afterwards in parentheses as "sonst" (meaning otherwise) or "angenommener" (meaning adopted).

Make a list of all known living members of your family, including even the most distant cousins, with their addresses. Then add to the list the names and addresses of old family friends if they are known to you.

Once this is done you can start to ask questions—in person, on the phone, and by mail. Write down everything you are told and be sure you also write down the name of the person who gave you the information—you may need to query an item with that person later on.

If by any chance you have an elderly aunt or great-aunt, this may be like striking the mother lode. Women are the custodians of family history—they know when and where people were born, they know who married whom and, in some cases, who *had* to marry whom! They know when people died and the cause of death. Remember, too, that they can tell you not only about the events of their own lives, but also about events they heard of from their grandparents. In the clear mind of an elderly person you may find 150 years of family history—a rich source of material just waiting to be uncovered.

When you are about to approach great-aunt Erika for help, please take care—particularly if you do not know her all that well and rarely visit her. Do not arrive unannounced with a tape recorder and a long list of prepared questions that you fire at her with military precision. If you do this you will get very little. Older people do not like tape recorders, and their minds, though quite clear, do not react instantly to a barrage of questions. Always make an appointment, explain what you are doing, tell them you will be grateful if they will share their knowledge and wisdom with you, and then go and see them with a small notebook, plus a supply of charm and patience. Then just sit and chat away like old friends, take notes quietly and unobtrusively, and you will learn a lot. Don't overtire them, and when you leave, say, "I would like to talk to you again. You have told me so many fascinating things. I want to come and see you again, and perhaps in the meantime you could jot down a note about any other things you remember." I guarantee that you will learn much more at the second visit than you do at the first! Of course, you will hear a lot of stories that are not of direct value to you, but if you have any sense of history you will benefit from these as well.

If you do have this elderly relative in your family, talk to him or her now—don't delay, don't put off going to see them. Almost every ancestor-hunter will say to you, "If only I had talked to my great-aunt and listened to her stories when she was alive. Now she is dead, and all her knowledge of the family went with her."

Ask everyone about everything you need to know—date of arrival in this country, name of the ship, port of arrival, occupation, religion, place of origin, place of death, place of burial, military service, date of naturalization—some of this information you will have already, some you will need to search hard for, but it will all help you along the road. So far as religion is concerned, a word of caution: coming from Germany, your family will probably be either Catholic or Evangelical Lutheran. Remember that people can change their religion—either through marriage, conversion, or happenstance. The latter could occur if your deeply religious ancestor settled in a place in this country where there was no Lutheran church. There might be a Methodist chapel, and so he might decide to attend services there. When a Lutheran church was built he would revert to his original denomination, but for a period of several years the vital events of the family may be recorded in the Methodist church registers.

I mentioned earlier the importance of talking to *every* member of your family. Just one member may have information unknown to anyone else. Let me tell you a story.

My wife was born in Scotland and so were her parents and grandparents and several generations beyond them. When she was a small child her grandfather mentioned to her that the family had come from England 200 years before. She remembered this, and many years later she commented about the story to her father. He told her there could not be any truth in it—the family was Scots way back forever (you must understand that if you are Scots and have English blood in your veins you keep quiet about it!).

When we started to trace my wife's family back we remembered grandfather's story and, without going into all the details, we found he was right to within twenty years. What is more, we traced the man who came from England and found a published family tree in a history book, which took us back to 1680 and gave us clues that eventually took us back to 1296. All because one member of a family was told something vital.

So some family stories are true, but many are not, and all stories should be treated with caution until you have proof as to their truth. I am not suggesting you are descended from Baron von Münchhausen but, let's be honest, over the years a certain amount of decoration can creep in. You may have been told about the Rhine castle I mentioned, but perhaps your ancestors only worked there, or were tenant farmers on the estate. You may have been told that great-grandfather was an officer in the Prussian army at the Battle of Sedan in 1870, whereas he was really a Feldwebel or sergeant.

When you start talking to members of your family you may meet with resistance from one or two who may say, "Leave well enough alone," "Let sleeping dogs lie," "Don't stir the pot, you don't know what will come to the top," and so on and so on. Try and overcome this sort of hindrance. They are probably afraid you will discover something to the discredit of the family, some rogue who stole a sheep, some skeleton in the closet. Maybe—horror of horrors!—great-grandfather was illegitimate. Who cares! Anyway, if it bothers you at all, remember you are not publishing your family tree in the local newspaper. It is very unlikely you will discover a bastard in your ancestry. So far as resistance is concerned, you must use all your well-known charm and tact—explain that even if there is something in the family background, you promise to say nothing about it to anyone else.

There is one other important thing you must never forget. Be sure you always send return postage when you write to anyone for information—even government departments overseas. If you do not, you may not get an answer. Remember you are not the only person writing for information. Tens of thousands of people are tracing their ancestors and writing letters, and most of them do not cover the cost of the return postage, so now the general rule has become "no postage no answer." You can do this by buying two International Reply Coupons from your local post office and enclosing them with your letter. You should also send a self-addressed airmail envelope, otherwise your reply may come by surface mail, and that has been known to take two months from Europe. The recipient can exchange your two coupons at a post office over there for enough stamps for an airmail reply. There is also another way to do it. If you know you will be settling down to quite a lot of correspondence with, let us say, Austria, then you can get a draft for ten dollars from your bank, mail it to the Direktor, Postamt, Vienna (Wien), Austria, with a letter saying, "I enclose a draft for ten dollars, please send me the equivalent value in Austrian stamps of the correct denomination for airmail postage to this country." This will save you about 40 percent of the cost compared with coupons.

When you are writing to archives, genealogical organizations, clergymen, officials of all kinds, remember they are not compelled to answer you. There is no international law that says they must. So be sure to write a nice, polite letter, give them as much background as you can about the subject of your inquiry, but make it brief and to the point, and thank them in advance for their kind assistance. The words "mit den besten Grüssen" before you sign your name can unlock many doors!

Quite apart from talking and writing to family members and friends, you must also search for family records of all kinds—letters, diaries, naturalization papers, family Bibles, family photograph albums, etc. A word of warning, though, about family Bibles. It was fashionable up until about 1900 to present one to a newly married couple so they could record the vital events of the new family—births and baptisms, and, eventually, marriages and deaths and burials. Special pages were provided for such records, either at the front of the Bible or between the Old and New Testaments. Often, people starting to trace their ancestors accept all the handwritten entries as "gospel," but "it ain't necessarily so," as Gershwin put it. If all the entries are in the same handwriting with no variation in style and neatness over more than two generations, the odds are that many entries were made long *after* the event and are, therefore, based on "hearsay" and are not reliable without other confirmation.

The family photograph album you possess is probably the most frustrating record you will find. There are all those lovely pictures of solemn-looking men and women who must be ancestors—but, unfortunately, no one has written their names below the photograph or on the back. Possibly your elderly relative can help to identify some of them for you. However, there is one clue in the album that may be of value to you. The chances are that the name and city of the photographer of any studio pictures will be printed or embossed on the front or back of them. If this same city is repeated several times, it is quite likely to be the place from which your immigrant ancestor came. He may have brought some of the photos with him, or they may have been sent out by the family he left behind—"Here is a photograph of your brother Heinrich and his new wife, Elisabeth." You can also use this clue of a possible place of origin in two other ways, both of which you are going to use anyway—first, to check if someone has already traced your family and, second, to try to find relatives still living in Europe.

This is what you must do:

1. *Has someone already traced your family back?* Write to the following organizations and ask them if they have any record of the family:

(a) The nearest branch of The Church of Jesus Christ of Latter-day Saints (the LDS Church). The church requires that its members trace their ancestors and, as a result, holds the largest collection of genealogical material in the world. This is described in detail later in this book.

(b) Write to the public library of the place in this country where your ancestor settled, and the library in the place from which he came (or you think he came). Write also to national, provincial, and local archives in the particular area in Europe. Get in touch with genealogical societies and family history societies in the same area.

In all these cases explain what you are doing and give as much information as you can about the sailing date, date of arrival in this country, place of settlement, religion, and occupation.

So far as local archives are concerned you should also give the name of the photographer named in your album and ask if he is still in business or, if he is not, whether his office records and original photographic plates have been given to the archives (this does happen occasionally and is worth inquiring about since you are writing anyway).

2. *How do you find out if you have living relatives in Europe?* Of course, you try to find this out from within your own family, but if you fail to discover anything, then there are two methods to use:

(a) If you know or believe your ancestor came from a particular small city or town or village, write a brief letter to the local newspaper. If your ancestor came from a big city like Berlin, Munich, or Vienna, the big dailies are unlikely to publish it—small-town or county papers will nearly always do so.

If you don't know the name of the local newspaper, it doesn't matter. Simply write to Der Redakteur, Die Zeitung, Nürnberg (or whatever is the name of the town or area in which you are interested). Your letter should be short and on the following lines:

My grandfather, Alois Furst, emigrated from your area in 1890. He was a farm worker. His father was named Johann. If there are any relatives still living in Nürnberg I would very much like to hear from them.

At this point you may be saying, "My grandfather emigrated a century ago—even if he left brothers and sisters behind, there will be no one alive to know about him." You are wrong! Do you realize that when grandfather emigrated this was the most shattering event ever to occur in his family? A son, a brother, was leaving home to cross the ocean to the other side of the world, never to be seen again. The event was, and is, unforgettable, and whenever this country is in the news someone over there will be saying, "Of course, grandfather had a brother who emigrated. We must have lots of cousins over there." They won't take any initiative to find *you*, but a letter to the local paper may help you find *them*!

(b) Another possible source of information is the telephone directory. If you have an uncommon German name, you should write to the embassy or nearest consulate of Germany, or whichever country is involved, and ask if they would be kind enough to photocopy the page in the local phone book for the place or area in which you are interested. If your name is Muller forget it! If it is Klippenhoffer then try it! The name must be uncommon, otherwise the method is not practical. Once you have your list of names and addresses—hopefully about twenty or thirty—then you can send a letter to the first five. If it brings no results then write to the next five, and so on. Here again, be brief and say:

> I saw your name in the phone book. My grandfather, Alois Furst, emigrated from your area in 1890. His father was named Johann. If you are descended from his brothers or sisters, or are in any way related to him, I would very much like to hear from you.

This is as good a place as any to talk about language. Of course, it is better if you can write all your letters of inquiry in German—to archives, to libraries, to churches, to newspapers, and to names in a phone book. However, if you have lost your ancestral language, try and get your letters translated by a family friend who speaks the language, by a local high school teacher, or by the local German society or organization. If all else fails, it is better to write in good English than in bad German.

You will probably get letters from people who are not related but are complete strangers going out of their way to help you. People all over the world are, generally speaking, kind and friendly—it is the other kind, unfortunately, who hit the headlines! Let me give you an example of what may happen to you—it happened to me.

My family originated in a remote valley in the Lake District of England. I have traced them back in a proven and continuous line to 1340, and from then with gaps to 1195. I have only visited the valley once, and that was many years ago. Last year I wrote a letter to the *Westmorland Gazette* (the local paper) asking if, by any chance, a reader had photographs of the houses and farms in which my ancestors had lived (I listed them) and, if so, could they lend me prints to be copied, or have them copied in England at my expense.

I had three replies from people who did not have any photographs but who had made special journeys to the valley to photograph the houses for me. One couple even made a fifty-foot movie of the valley for me. So try letters to newspapers.

Now, one final word of advice before we move on to German history. I mentioned above that you should contact family history societies for information as to whether anyone has already traced, or is tracing, your family. You should also give some thought to becoming a member of the organization covering the district from whence your ancestors came, providing that you are not experiencing language problems. The various societies are listed in this book. There are several good reasons for joining such a society:

1. It publishes a newsletter at regular intervals and you will obtain a great deal of information about the area and its genealogical records.

2. It will keep you up-to-date as to new sources of information, and old ones that have just reappeared after many missing years.

3. It will publish your queries in the newsletter free of charge.

4. It lists the names and addresses of members and the names for which they are searching.

If you are interested in Germans from the Palatinate there is a society, and if you are interested in Germans from Prussia there is a society for that area, too. They are all listed later on.

There have been important changes in the German Postal Code system. Before unification the postal codes for each location had the prefix O or W to distinguish between East and West Germany. All numbers were four digit. Now there is a new five-digit code applicable to the whole country. You will find the new codes in all addresses in this book. It is very important you use the postal code because of the duplication of place-names in the country. There are, for example, a dozen places named Königsberg! Some of them are tiny villages.

THE GERMANS AND GERMANY

If we think about our German ancestry, it is easy to be led astray by lack of knowledge of the original Germanic tribes and their descendants. Without this knowledge it is difficult to avoid making mistakes that may delay or even halt forever our search for our German roots.

When we read about German colonies we only find mention of Tanganyika, Southwest Africa, the Cameroons, and Western Samoa, but over many centuries the hardy and adventurous German race has, in fact, colonized many parts of Europe.

A number of different tribes formed the German race more than a thousand years ago—Franks, Bavarians, Saxons, and Swabians, to mention only a few of them. Today, German is the mother tongue of 100 million people.

The development and coalescence of the German nation took many centuries. The word "Deutsch" (German) was first used in the eighth century, but it only referred to the spoken language of the area known as eastern Franconia. This empire reached its height of importance under the Emperor Charlemagne (Karl der Grosse), and after his death in 814 it disintegrated. The western section eventually became the area we now know as France. The eastern section varied in area over the centuries, but the main area—the heartland—became known as the Deutschland (the land of the Germans). By 911 the Duke of Franconia was elected King of the Franks, and later King of the Romans. By the eleventh century the area became known as the Roman Empire, and by the thirteenth the Holy Roman Empire. In the fifteenth century the words "German Nation" were added.

Before and during all these dynastic and political events, the German tribes overran most of the original Roman Empire as far east as the Elbe—beyond it were the fierce Slavic tribes. During this period the tribes took firm root in what we now know as Switzerland, Liechtenstein, Austria, northern Italy, the Netherlands, and the Baltic states. They were also invited into Transylvania by the Hungarian king in

1150. Siebenburgen—the German name for Transylvania—derives from the seven fortified towns established by the Germans. Although they came from the Rhine and Moselle area, they were known as "Saxons." There were some 5,000 settlers who were given as much land as they could cultivate and allowed to retain their own customs and language. Some did not stay long but moved south into the area known as the Banat, or west into Hungary proper. After eight centuries their descendants are still in Transylvania. However, there are now only some half-million of them, since the rest fled to Germany when the Communists took over after the Second World War.

While all this was going on, the Order of the Teutonic Knights and the Livonian Brothers of the Sword were extending German power into the Baltic countries of Estonia, Latvia, and Lithuania. The Teutonic Knights were formed originally to take part in the Crusades, but eventually settled in Prussia in 1309, and then extended their power and influence eastward into Livonia and Courland. At the same time King Andrew II of Hungary called on the Teutonic Knights to protect Transylvania from the Cumans and the Mongols in the east. So both northeastern and southeastern Europe were "colonized" by the Germans. The prime aim of the Knights was conquest and loot, but behind them came settlers, bringing a predominant German influence into the conquered territories. The Drive to the East (Drang nach Osten) started with Charlemagne's armies and the Teutonic Knights, and ended with Hitler.

During this period there were also smaller migrations to Schlesien (Silesia), which is now divided between the Czech Republic and Poland, and to Bessarabia—until 1945 Romanian and now in Moldova. In the reign of the empress Maria Theresa of Austria (1740–1780) many Germans—the so-called Danubian Swabians—migrated to four areas of Hungary: Bacska, the Banat, the Kingdom of Croatia, and part of Slovakia. A number of these settlers later moved on into Ukraine, Bessarabia, and other areas of southern Russia. Others—like the Zipsers—settled in Slovakia.

After the First Partition of Poland in 1772, Frederick the Great of Prussia (1740–1786) settled West Prussia and the area around Bromberg with German immigrants from Württemberg and Baden-Durlach. Said the king, "Get me farmers from Württemberg and the economic misery will come to an end."

In the middle of the eighteenth century the empress Catherine the Great of Russia (1762–1796) invited all foreigners who possessed skills of some kind to come to her country as settlers and colonists. In cases of financial hardship the cost of transportation was paid. In addition, all settlers received a loan of money toward the cost of building a house and buying livestock and farm or trade equipment—with repayment required in ten years.

The proclamation of the empress was distributed throughout Europe but did not meet with any great response except in the Germanic area and, to a much smaller degree, Sweden. Most of the colonists came from Hesse (Hessen) and the Rhineland, but all German-speaking areas were represented in varying numbers.

I must quote to you the titles of the empress as set out in her proclamation. No, it will not help your genealogical research one little bit, but I found it amusing and so, I hope, will you:

> Empress and Autocrat of all the Russians at Moscow, Kiev, Vladimir, Novgorod, Czarina of Kazan, Czarina of Astrachan, Czarina of Siberia, Lady of Plaskow, Grand Duchess of Smolensko, Duchess of Estonia and Livland, Carelia, Twer, Yogoria, Permia, Viatka, and Bulgaria and others; Lady and Grand Duchess of Novgorod in the Netherland of Chernigov, Resan, Rostov, Yaroslav, Belooseria, Udoria, Obdoria, Condonia, and Ruler of the entire North Region and Lady of the Yurish, of the Cartalinian and Grusinian czars, and the Cabardinian land, of the Cherkessian and Gorisian princes, and the lady of the manor and sovereign of many others.

The areas opened up for settlement by the empress were underpopulated and open to frequent attacks by the Ottoman Turks. The Germans, for their part, were eager to settle for a variety of reasons. Germany as we know it today did not exist. It was a vast conglomeration of 1789 kingdoms, principalities, grand duchies, dukedoms, electorates, free states, and free cities—down to tiny independent states of a few hectares. Men were dragged off into various warring armies, women and children were raped or killed or both, agriculture was ruined by the constant wars, and people starved. There was also religious persecution, high taxes, civil disturbances, and in many areas a high population density. Life was miserable and dangerous for the ordinary people, and it was no wonder the grass in the next field looked much greener.

If your family is descended from the Germans who emigrated to Russia between the mid-1700s and the mid-1800s, you may have assumed there is no chance of tracing your forebears back to their place of origin in the area that is now Germany. In fact, there is a very good chance records exist that will give you vital information.

Between 1804 and 1842 over 72,000 people emigrated to Russia, and estimates for the entire period range as high as 150,000 from the German area alone. It was one of the great mass movements of history. For a century they poured into Russia and established themselves in fairly close areas of settlement in the Volga region, the Black Sea area, and the Caucasus.

The whole story is documented in a remarkable book by a very remarkable man—Dr. Karl Stumpp. It is entitled *The Emigration from*

Germany to Russia 1763–1862 and was published in 1978 by the American Historical Society of Germans from Russia, 631 D Street, Lincoln, NE 68502. It lists the names of some 50,000 German settlers, with their places of origin and settlement.

It may be helpful to quote the areas of origin and settlement over the century:

Period of Emigration	*Place of Origin*	*Area of Settlement*
1763–68	Hessen, Rheinland, Pfalz, Sachsen, Württemberg, Switzerland	Volga (E and L)
1765	Sulzfeld, Württemberg	Reibensdorf (E)
1766	Hessen, Württemberg, Brandenburg	Petersburg, Black Sea
1766	Hessen	Belowesh (E and C)
1780	Preussen, Württemberg, Bayern	Josefstal, Fischerdorf, Jamburg, in Dnieper area
1782	Sweden	Schwedendorf (E)
1786	Preussen	Alt-Danzig
1789–90	Danzig, West Preussen	Chortitza (M)
1804–6	Alsace, Pfalz, Baden	Franzfeld, Mariental, Josefstal, by Odessa (C)
1804–6	Württemberg, Alsace, Pfalz, Baden, Hungary	Grossliebental, Neuburg, Alexanderhilf
1804–6	Danzig, West Preussen	Halbstadt, Molotschna (M)
1804–6	Württemberg, Baden, Hessen	Prischib, Molotschna (E and C)
1804–6	Württemberg, Switzerland	Neusatz, Zürichtal, in the Crimea (E and C)
1808–10	Württemberg, Alsace, Pfalz	Bergdorf, Glückstal, Kassel, Neudorf, by Odessa (E)
1808–10	Alsace, Baden, Poland	Baden, Elsass, Kandel, Selz, Mannheim, Strassburg (C)
1808–10	Alsace, Baden, Pfalz, Württemberg	Beresan and Odessa (C)
1812–27	Württemberg, Baden, Hessen	Prischib, Molotschna (E)
1814–16	Württemberg, Preussen, Bayern, and Poland	Bessarabia, and near Odessa
1817–18	Württemberg	South Caucasus (E)
1821–34	Württemberg, Preussen, Bayern, and Poland	Bessarabia, and near Odessa
1822–31	Württemberg	Swabian colonies near Berdjansk (E)

Period of Emigration	Place of Origin	Area of Settlement
1823–42	Danzig, West Preussen, Baden, Hessen, Rheinland	Grunau area (E and C)
1853 and	Danzig, West Preussen	Samara (M)
1859–62	(This was the last emigration from Germany)	

(E=Evangelical, L=Lutheran, C=Catholic, M=Mennonite)

When the German armies invaded the USSR in 1941 they were welcomed by the majority of the Germans living in Ukraine. When the Wehrmacht retreated in 1942 many of the German settlers left too, fearing reprisals from the Red Army, and they were wise. They made their way back to Germany, the fatherland their ancestors had left more than a century before, and those left behind in Ukraine were killed or imprisoned.

Millions of Germans in other areas of Europe became refugees after the Second World War. In 1945 Czechoslovakia regained the Sudetenland. This German-speaking area had been taken from Austria in 1919. In 1938 it was reunited with Germany. After 1945 the three and a half million German inhabitants were expelled and their property and possessions confiscated. Other refugees from Poland and the USSR brought the total number of Germans returning home to over thirteen million.

Quite apart from the mass movements of population shown above, there was, of course, a continual movement to and fro between the multitude of German states before and after unification in 1871. Most of these movements of individuals were recorded, and the records are in the various state archives. If a man wished to move from Hannover to Brunswick, for example, he would notify the Hannover police of his impending departure and his destination. On arrival in Brunswick he had to report to the police within three days. They, in turn, notified the Hannover police that he had arrived.

Although these tremendous upheavals will have a major effect on your ancestor-hunting, you must also become aware of other problems ahead. For example, there are 23,000 Germans still in Denmark, 100,000 in Belgium, over a million in Alsace (Elsass), and 26,000 German speakers in the South Tirol—now in Italy.

In addition, you must consider the "lost territories" of Germany and what has happened to their genealogical records. These territories consist of the following areas:

To Belgium: In 1919 Eupen, Malmédy, and Moresnet
To Czechoslovakia: In 1945 the western part of Silesia (Schlesien)
To Denmark: In 1920 North Schleswig
To France: In 1919 Alsace (Elsass)

To Poland:	In 1945 the eastern parts of Brandenburg, Pomerania (Pommern), the southern part of East Prussia (Ostpreussen), Posen, the western part of Silesia (Schlesien), West Prussia (Westpreussen), and Danzig
To the USSR:	In 1945 the northern part of East Prussia (Ostpreussen) and Memel

The genealogical records for these areas are located in the various archives listed below:

Belgium: Church and civil records of the transferred area are in the Provincial Archives at Liège (Archives de l'État à Liège, rue Pouplin 8, 4000 Liège).

Czech Republic: The two major cities from Silesia now in this country are Leitmeritz (now Litoměřice) and Troppau (now Opava). The addresses of the two archives are:

Statní Oblastní Archiv
Dominikánsky Kláster
Krajiska 1, 41274 Litoměřice

Statní Oblastní Archiv
Demovni ulice 1, Opava

Denmark: The old Duchy of Schleswig-Holstein was divided in 1920. The northern part went to Denmark and the southern part remained German. Records for the latter part are in the Landesarchiv Schleswig-Holstein, Schloss Gottorf, 24837 Schleswig, Germany. The census records for the area lost by Germany are located in the Landsarkivet for de sønderjyske Landsdele, Haderslevvej 45, 6200 Aabenraa, Denmark. The church records for the northern part are also in these archives, as are copies of some of the Holstein records.

France: Genealogical records for Alsace-Lorraine are in the Archives Départementales du Bas-Rhin, 5-9 rue Fischart, 67000 Strasbourg (for the French section, or Lorraine) and in Staatsarchiv, Karmeliterstrasse 1-3, 56068 Koblenz, Germany (for Alsace-Elsass).

Poland: The country is divided into counties (voivods) and each has its own archives. Those of the following cities and the area around them are in these various archives. The original German name is given first and the new Polish name is in parentheses. Inquiries should be sent to Wojewódskie Archiwum Państowe, followed by the postal code and the city or town name in Polish:

Allenstein	(10074 Olsztyn)
Breslau	(50215 Wrocław)
Bromberg	(85009 Bydgoszcz)

Danzig	(80958 Gdańsk)
Grünberg	(66002 Zielona Góra)
Kattowitz	(40950 Katowice)
Köslin	(75601 Koszalin)
Oppeln	(45016 Opole)
Pless	(43200 Pszczyna)
Posen	(61744 Poznań)
Schneidemühl	(64920 Piła)
Stettin	(70410 Szczecin)
Thorn	(87100 Toruń)

(There are still 750,000 Germans living in Poland.)

Russia and the Former USSR: Church and civil records do exist for former areas of Germany or German settlements. Some Memel Church records are in the State Archives of Lithuania (see next page). In addition, both these archives and those of Estonia hold many records of German settlement in those countries. The archivists of all three Baltic states are now very helpful to ancestor-hunters overseas.

Russia itself and, to a lesser degree, Ukraine and Belarus are making moves to open their archives to genealogical research. However, I do not want to give the impression that all this will happen in the immediate future. My own visits to archives in Russia make me very pessimistic. The will to help is there but the finances and facilities are not.

There are some records of genealogical interest in the National Archives in Washington, D.C. I have not seen them myself but I understand the following are available:

Records of the Reichkommissar for the Baltic States 1941–45 (Microfilm T 459, rolls 3, 11, and 12).

Records of the Reich Ministry for the Occupied Eastern Territories 1941–45 (Microfilm T 454, rolls 1, 2, 3, 16, and 107).

These two series were microfilmed by the U.S. government at the end of World War II and contain details about archives in the Baltic states and Belarus. They include the records of the Civil Registry Offices (ZAGS) and a number of parish registers. There are no indexes to these records. The originals are in the Staatsarchiv, Karmeliterstrasse 1-3, 56068 Koblenz, Germany.

The state archives in the newly independent Baltic states of Estonia, Latvia, and Lithuania also contain Lutheran and Catholic church registers as well as civil registration records from 1919. The addresses of the archives are given below.

Estonia. The State Archives are located at Maneeźi 4, 200102 Tallinn. Church registers and civil registration of births, marriages, and deaths up to 1926 are in the State Registry Office, Lossi plats 1a, 200103 Tallinn.

Latvia. There are three state archives in this country. The Central State History Archives (Slokas ielā 16, 226007 Riga) holds records of the pre-Soviet period. The Central State Archives (Bezdeligu ielā 1, 226007 Riga) has records of the Soviet occupation period. The Central State Cine-phono-photo Documents Archives (Skuni ielā 11, 226007 Riga) is also of interest to genealogists.

Lithuania. There are three state archives of interest to genealogists. The State Parish Register Archives (Lietuvos valstybinis metriku archyvas, 21 Kalinausko, Vilnius); the State Archives (Lietuvos valstybinis archyvas, 21 Kareiviu, Vilnius), which has birth, marriage, and death registers, wills, and land records; and the Historical State Archives (Lietuvos valstybinis istorijos archyvas, 10 Gerosios Vilites, Vilnius).

The chief archivists of all three countries have assured me of their willingness to be of all possible help to overseas inquirers. A reasonable fee will be charged. You may also visit the various archives and do your own search.

Germany only existed as an undivided country from 1871 until 1945— in contrast with England and France, which had been unified for more than five centuries. Systems of government in the various German states ranged from absolute monarchies to the near-democracy of some of the electorates and free cities. Various forms of confederation or economic grouping took hold, flowered for a few years, and died. Each state had its own laws, archives, and system of recording events. You cannot say, for example, that "censuses were first held in Germany in 1871." That is true for the unified Germany, but censuses were taken in Württemberg in 1821, in Baden in 1852, and so on. The only unified force in the Germanic area was the church—first the Catholic and later the Lutheran.

By the middle of the nineteenth century the number of self-governing German states had been reduced to thirty-four. Some of these formed the German Confederation, which also included Austria—still trying to assert its position as leader of the German people. However, the alliance was a shaky one because of the emerging power of Prussia, under the leadership of the great Bismarck. The two rivals did join together in an attack on Denmark in 1866 and seized Schleswig-Holstein, which they divided between them. A few months later they quarreled over the "spoils" and Prussia took over the whole territory. At this point Austria withdrew from the German Confederation and joined with Hungary in 1867 to form the Austro-Hungarian Empire.

The German Confederation was then renamed the North German

Confederation under the leadership of Prussia, and included all the states north of the River Main. The eastern boundary was extended as far as Memel. In 1871, following a short and successful war against France, Prussia persuaded the southern states to join the Confederation with its new name of German Empire (Deutsches Reich). The king of Prussia was then proclaimed emperor on January 16, 1871. Suddenly, in the very center of Europe, a most powerful new country existed, and for the first time in over a thousand years the German people were one nation under strong leadership.

In the short period of a quarter of a century the German people had developed a pride in their nation, which was strong enough to overcome the hatreds and mistrusts of a thousand years of division and despair.

The new empire included the following territory:

(a) Kingdoms of Bavaria, Prussia, Saxony, and Württemberg;

(b) Grand Duchy of Baden;

(c) Free Cities of Bremen, Hamburg, and Lübeck, and Anhalt, Brunswick, Darmstadt, Hesse, Lippe, Mecklenburg, Oldenburg, Reuss, and the various states comprising Thuringia. (Justice, education, health, and police were left under the control of the individual states.)

During the period of unification between 1871 and 1945, little or no attempt was made to centralize records in one place such as the capital, Berlin. Instead, they remained in the capital cities of the original states. In retrospect, this was a blessing to ancestor-hunters because the destruction of German records during the Second World War was surprisingly small. Imagine what would have happened if everything had been in Berlin!

Details have already been given of the post-war dismemberment of Germany and the transfer of territory to Czechoslovakia, Poland, and the USSR. The remaining part of Germany was then divided into the eastern half, occupied by the USSR, and the western half, occupied by Britain, Belgium, France, and the United States. These two parts later became the German Democratic Republic (Deutsche Demokratische Republik, or D.D.R.) and the Federal Republic of Germany (Bundesrepublik Deutschland, or B.R.D.). Details of the division were:

D.D.R.: Anhalt, Brandenburg (western part), part of Brunswick (Braunschweig), Mecklenburg-Schwerin, Mecklenburg-Strelitz, Reuss, Sachsen-Altenburg, Sachsen-Meiningen, Sachsen-Weimar, Schwarzburg-Rudolstadt, and Schwarzburg-Sondershausen. Also four provinces of the State of Prussia (the parts remaining after territory taken by the three countries mentioned above).

B.R.D.: Baden, Bavaria (Bayern), part of Brunswick (Braunschweig), Coburg, Lippe, Oldenburg, Schaumberg-Lippe, part of Thuringia

(Thüringen), Waldeck, Westphalia (Westfalen), and Württemberg; and five provinces of the State of Prussia—Hanover (Hannover), Hessen-Nassau, Rhineland (Rheinland), Schleswig-Holstein, and Sigmaringen.

After the division of Germany in 1945 various changes were made in each section of the country, and they were administered as follows:

D.D.R.: Originally this consisted of five provinces (Länder). These were abolished and replaced by fifteen districts (Kreise). However, the D.D.R., unlike the B.R.D., was not a federal state, and all power was centered in the capital (East, or Ost, Berlin).

B.R.D.: Originally this consisted of ten federal states (Bundesländer, or just Länder): Baden-Württemberg, Bavaria (Bayern), Bremen (city-state), Hamburg (city-state), Hesse (Hessen), Lower Saxony (Niedersachsen), North Rhine-Westphalia (Nordrhein-Westfalen), Rhineland-Palatinate (Rheinland-Pfalz), Saarland, and Schleswig-Holstein. The city-state of Berlin (West) was integrated into the legal and economic system of the Federal Republic. The republic was further divided into twenty-five administrative areas (Regierungsbezirke), 327 counties or districts (Kreise), and about 8,500 municipalities.

The sixteen areas of the unified country and their capital cities are:

Baden-Württemberg (Stuttgart)
Bayern (Munich/München)
Berlin
Brandenburg (Potsdam)*
Bremen
Hamburg
Hessen (Wiesbaden)
Mecklenburg-Vorpommern (Schwerin)*
Niedersachsen (Hannover)
Nordrhein-Westfalen (Düsseldorf)
Rheinland-Pfalz (Mainz)
Saarland (Saarbrücken)
Sachsen (Dresden)*
Sachsen-Anhalt (Magdeburg)*
Schleswig-Holstein (Kiel)
Thüringen (Erfurt)*

The Länder marked with an asterisk (*) are the new political divisions of the area previously known as East Germany. They replace the fifteen districts (Bezirkes) mentioned on the previous page. The names of the districts within each of the five Länder are:

BRANDENBURG: Berlin, Cottbus, Frankfurt, Potsdam

MECKLENBURG-VORPOMMERN: Neubrandenburg, Rostock, Schwerin
SACHSEN: Dresden, Chemnitz (formerly Karl-Marx-Stadt), Leipzig
SACHSEN-ANHALT: Halle, Magdeburg
THÜRINGEN: Erfurt, Gera, Suhl

THE CONTINUING MIGRATION

Earlier in this book I wrote about the great Germanic migrations in the Middle Ages and in the eighteenth and nineteenth centuries. After World War II thirteen million Germans left their homes in other European countries and found refuge in the Fatherland. Now, with the unification of Germany and free emigration from the former Soviet Union and Eastern Europe, a new wave of migration is bringing more Germans back to Germany. It has been forgotten (except by those who suffer) that some two million Germans still live in the former Soviet Union— in European Russia itself, and Ukraine, Kazakhstan, and Siberia. Many thousands more are still living in Poland and Romania.

The Germans in Kazakhstan may number as many as a million— some descended from the Germans who originally settled in the Volga Basin at the invitation of Catherine the Great, and others who were exiled from Ukraine by Stalin.

If you know you have German relatives in the former Soviet Union, Poland, or Romania you may be able to make contact through the International Red Cross or the Immigration Ministry in Bonn.

STARTING THE FAMILY TREE

❧

So—you have read the previous pages and your interest in your German ancestry has been aroused or rekindled. What *do* you do now?

You buy a large sheet of white paper (about three by two feet) from a stationer or an art store, plus a three-ring binder. At the bottom of the sheet of paper you write your name and those of your brothers and sisters, if any, and any children. You also include dates and places of birth, marriage, and death. You write the names of your brothers and sisters in a horizontal line in descending order of age.

I am inventing an entirely imaginary Joseph Furst, whose family on both sides originated in "Germany," but he doesn't know when they emigrated or where they came from. He has often wondered about his German background but he has never got down to doing anything about it—mainly because he has no idea how to start, and also because he is afraid it may cost a lot of money.

When you have the names of your brother and sister written down, you add the dates of all the vital events (that is what we call births, marriages, and deaths) for them and their children and yours. The start of your family tree will look like the one on the following page for the imaginary Furst family:

JOSEPH	WILLIAM	ANNA
Born: 8 June 1920	Born: 13 January 1922	Born: 2 February 1924
Townsville WI	Townsville WI	Townsville WI
= Mary Johnson	= Catherine Spaak	= Herbert Whittaker
(4 July 1947 Madison)	(3 May 1944 Racine)	(23 March 1950 Avon)

JOHN	ERICA	MARIA	RICHARD	HERBERT
Born: 4 April 1949	Born: 3 Feb 1950	Born: 2 Jan 1945	Born: 11 Nov 1951	Born: 11 Nov 1951
= Bridget May (18 June 1975 Buffalo NY)	unmarried	= Mario Donizetti (4 May 1965 New York NY)	unmarried	= Mary Adams (1 April 1974 Philadelphia PA)

PATRICK	MAUREEN	CESARE	MARIA	RICHARD
Born: 11 Aug 1976 Madison	Born: 4 Dec 1978 Madison	Born: 3 Mar 1966 Ithaca NY	Born: 2 Nov 1968 Ithaca NY	Born: 27 May 1976 Fargo ND

Next, you write in above all these entries the information you have about your mother and father:

JOHANN FURST		ERIKA BRAND
Born: 3 December 1895	=	Born: 4 August 1896
Milwaukee WI		Krefeld, Germany

(married on 5 May 1918 in the
Evangelical-Lutheran Church,
Milwaukee)

(*Note:* Always enter dates as they appear above—8/6/1920 can mean June 8 in one country and August 6 in another.)

Now your family tree is growing, and you turn your attention to your grandparents. At this stage you must decide whether you only want to trace the Furst family back or whether you prefer to trace the Brands, or both. There is no rule about this—you make the decision. If you decide to trace both the Fursts and the Brands, I suggest you deal with one family at a time. You will find it much easier to remember names and places as you go along. Of course, you will be writing everything down, but it is still better to concentrate on one side at a time. If you are looking down a long list of names one surname will spring out at you, whereas if you are looking for three or four you may easily miss one entry. An exception to this suggestion is if both your grandparents came from the same place—in that case, of course, you trace both families at the same time. However, you know your father was born in Milwaukee and your mother in Germany. It is easier to use the records here to start with, so father comes first.

Your sister reminds you that your father once said his father and mother spoke German to each other when they wanted to keep secrets, but that they both spoke English fluently but with an accent. This information does not help you very much—they may have been born in Germany or their German accents may have been because they spoke German at home as children, even though they were born here. You can never take anything for granted in ancestor-hunting—nor should you ever jump to a conclusion without checking for supporting evidence.

You have come up against your first obstacle. Was grandfather born in the United States or not? If he was German-born, where did he come from? Perhaps it wasn't in Germany at all. It is very likely he was born before 1871 (your father was born in 1895), and Germany did not exist as a separate country until that year.

How can you answer these questions? Your only living relatives here—apart from the next generation—are your brother and sister, and they have told you all they know, so what do you have? You know your own father was born in Milwaukee, and you have a copy of his birth certificate, which tells you his father's name was Josef Furst. Your father was born in 1895, and you remember he once told you he was only eight when his father died. So now you know you want to find out about a Josef Furst who was alive in 1895 and dead by 1903. You also know from the same certificate that his mother was Maria (née Ziegler). From the same source you know that Josef and Maria were living at 68 Heath Street, Milwaukee, when your father was born.

You write to the Section of Vital Statistics in Madison, Wisconsin and tell them you want a copy of the marriage certificate of Josef Furst and Maria Ziegler—believed to have been married in Milwaukee between 1890 and 1895. Of course, you don't know yet if the event did take place there or not, but your checking must start somewhere. They will probably send you a form to complete and will tell you the fee required.

In due course you receive a letter telling you that a search of the marriage records for the period specified does not show an entry for the marriage. Now you know the odds are that the marriage took place in Germany. What is the next step? Census returns! These were taken on a statewide basis in Wisconsin from 1855 to 1905 and are now in the custody of the State Historical Society in Madison. You write to them, enclosing a self-addressed stamped envelope, and ask for details of the 1895 census return for 68 Heath Street, Milwaukee. For a small fee you will have opened up a whole new area of searching, and created new problems:

68 Heath Street Milwaukee

JOSEF FURST	age 38	Lutheran	Born Germany
MARIA FURST	age 37	Lutheran	Born Germany
JOHANN FURST	infant	Lutheran	Born Milwaukee

There are many other sources that can provide help—newspapers, passenger lists, land grants, etc. These will be found in various archives in Washington and individual states and cities. Many are available on microfilm and can be borrowed through, and read in, your local library. In addition to these, you have church records and registers of the different denominations, which are in the individual churches or in the various church archives. These are usually located in the city where a bishop has his headquarters. There are also tombstones in churchyards and in public burial grounds which exist in most areas. Don't forget early newspapers (which often listed emigrants leaving the city or area), local histories (often only in manuscript form), and directories of inhabitants.

Last, but most certainly not least, is the vast collection of genealogical records acquired by The Church of Jesus Christ of Latter-day Saints (the LDS Church), formerly known as the Mormon Church. You will find much more about these records later in this book. They do, in fact, include many of the official records I mentioned above.

One vital thing you must do is find out if someone—perhaps some unknown fifth or sixth cousin—has already traced your ancestors. You should contact the nearest LDS family history center and the public libraries and archives in the area from whence your ancestor came, and also in the area in which he or she settled. Make contact, too, with genealogical societies in the same areas. It would be a major tragedy if you were to spend a couple of years and, perhaps, a couple of hundred dollars tracing back your forebears, only to discover the search had already been made and you had never checked!

Let me give you an example of what may happen. Some years ago my wife and I decided to trace her grandmother's side of the family in Scotland—the name was Copland. We already had the information for four generations back, but beyond that all we knew was that the family had been living in the area of a city named Dumfries, in the southwest of Scotland. We were in the country at that time on a visit, and so we went to Dumfries prepared to spend a couple of weeks there visiting churchyards, churches, and so on. First of all, though, we went to the local library, met the librarian, and asked him, "Do you, by any chance, have any information about a family named Copland which used to be prominent in this area a century and a half ago?" "Oh, yes," he replied. "I have a great deal of information about the family." He then produced a 400-page typed history of the family written by a family member fifty years earlier!

It was complete in every detail. The author had done his research most thoroughly, and had meticulously recorded the source of all his information. Within thirty minutes we had found just where my wife's branch of the family fitted into the family history. From then on all the work had been done and there was a complete record of the family—documented and proved—back to a man named Ulf the Viking, Lord of Copeland, who had been alive in 1135. This took my wife's ancestry back twenty-four generations! If we had not checked with the library it would have taken us several years to go back that far. We also found that we were twenty-second cousins, or something like that, since I am descended from that same Viking through my Curwen ancestors.

Enough of the Baxters and the Coplands—let us go back to the Furst family. What are the basic facts you have to go on in your search in Germany? You know from the census return that both your grandparents were born in Germany in 1857 and 1858 respectively—but Germany did not exist until 1871. How can you find out exactly where they were born? Suddenly, you remember that often the place of birth was put on a tombstone. You know they died in Milwaukee and that your grandfather died about 1903. You get in touch with the office of the old public burial ground there and ask if they can possibly look at their records, see if your grandparents were buried there, and, if so, if any place of birth appears on the tombstone. You realize, of course, that the odds are against you—they may have been buried elsewhere, there may be no information on the tombstone, it may not be possible to decipher the lettering, the staff of the burial ground may not be helpful.

You wait and wait for several weeks and then you get your answer.

> We have checked our records and find that on lot 39, avenue H46, is located the grave of Josef Furst and his wife, Maria. According to our records the information supplied by Mr. Furst's widow stated he had died on 12 May 1903, aged 46, and was interred on 16 May. Cause of death accidental. The grave also contains the remains of Mrs. Maria Furst (née Ziegler) who died 17 July 1916, and was interred on 21 July. Cause of death heart failure. Age 58. Information supplied by next of kin (son) Johann Furst. A member of the staff has visited the grave site and it appears that Mr. Furst was born in Erlangen, Germany, in 1857, and Mrs. Furst in Nürnberg, Germany, in 1858.

Before you write to the church authorities in Germany you should check with the nearest LDS family history center. The church has an ongoing project to copy all kinds of records of genealogical value in

Germany. It may or may not have copied church records in the two places mentioned on the tombstone. If the registers have been microfilmed, you can borrow them through an LDS family history center and search them yourself there when the microfilms arrive from Salt Lake City. It is possible, too, that the church may have a computer printout of all Furst entries in the various Nürnberg church registers. The odds are against this being so, but check anyway.

If you are going to sit down and search the registers on microfilm yourself, you must be prepared for bad writing, faint writing, and, worst of all, the old Germanic script. There are several books available that explain script and German symbols used in the registers. I mentioned one of them at the beginning of this book, but there are others, and the library itself probably has at least one of them available.

If the LDS Church has not copied the church registers, you should now write to Germany—but where, you may ask, are Erlangen and Nürnberg? You should visit your nearest large library and look up a good indexed map of Germany. If you cannot find one, write to the nearest German embassy or consulate and they will tell you. Don't forget the return postage and a self-addressed envelope! Either way, you will soon discover that Nürnberg is a large city in Bayern (Bavaria) and Erlangen a small town just outside. For the purpose of this particular example of a search, I have made the Fursts Evangelical-Lutherans, but they could just as easily have been Catholics—the procedure is the same.

Write to the Pastor (Herr Pfarrer), Evangelische-Lutherische Kirche, Erlangen. Cover the return postage, enclose a self-addressed airmail envelope, and offer to pay the fees required. I cannot guarantee the amount, but it is unlikely to exceed five dollars. Try and get your letter translated into German, and arrange for the reply to be translated as well. If you cannot do this then write in English. Be brief, be clear, be polite, and be grateful in advance:

Sehr geehrter Herr Pfarrer
I will be most grateful if you can check your register and let me know if you have a record of the baptism of Josef Furst between 1855 and 1860. If so, may I have a copy of the entry with all the details of parents, witnesses, addresses, etc., if they are given. I will pay whatever fee is required and thank you in advance for your kind assistance. A self-addressed envelope and two International Reply Coupons are enclosed.

Because Maria Ziegler came from Nürnberg, a big city with several churches, your letter will be worded differently and will go to the Sekretär, Landeskirchliches Archiv (Veilhofstrasse 28, 90489 Nürnberg)—these archives include material from most of the Evangelical-Lutheran churches in Nürnberg. In this case your letter will read:

> Sehr geehrter Herr Sekretär
>
> My grandmother, Maria Ziegler, was born in Nürnberg between 1857 and 1860. Unfortunately I do not know her address or the name of her parents, but I do know she was a member of the Evangelical-Lutheran Church. I think there are probably several churches in Nürnberg and will be most grateful if you can possibly ask the pastors of the churches to check their registers for her baptism. If the entry can be found I would like a copy with all the details of parents, witnesses, addresses, etc. if they are given. I will pay whatever fee is required and thank you in advance for your kind assistance. A self-addressed envelope and two International Reply Coupons are enclosed.

Let us be optimistic and assume all goes well and you obtain all the information for which you asked. From this point you go steadily back via the marriage of the parents of Josef and Maria—through church registers and all the many other sources of information that are described in the following pages.

THE RECORDS OF THE
LDS CHURCH

❧

Anyone starting to trace his or her ancestors must make use of the vast genealogical collection of The Church of Jesus Christ of Latter-day Saints (the LDS Church), formerly known as the Mormons. If you are tracing your German ancestors the LDS Church may be very valuable to you. It is not necessary to be a member of the church, or even to approve of its teachings, to be able to use its records.

Occasionally people have understandable fears about making contact with the church in their ancestor-hunt. They are afraid efforts will be made to convert them, and that an LDS elder may turn up on their doorstep one day to try to bring this about. This is not going to happen. The members of the church are extraordinarily nice, kind, helpful people, and your temporary association with them will do you no harm. I am not an LDS Church member, but over a great many years I have learned to appreciate their good qualities and the help I have received from many of them.

The interest of church members in genealogy stems from their theological belief that family relationships and family associations are intended to be eternal, and not limited to a short period of mortal existence. Church members "sealed together" are not married only "until death do you part." It is believed that a husband and wife and their children remain together throughout eternity as a family unit with their ancestors and descendants.

Members of the church collect genealogical information about their ancestors in order to perform "sealing ceremonies" in temples erected for that purpose. Before the sealing of families from generation to generation can be performed, the families must be properly identified. This is done by members' own personal research and by using the records of the church—in particular the extraordinary collection of the Family History Library of The Church of Jesus Christ of Latter-day Saints (as it is officially known), located at 35 North West Temple, Salt Lake City, UT 84150.

The church is engaged in the most active and comprehensive genealogical program ever known. Microfilm is the heart of the operation, and trained specialists are microfilming records every day in some fifty countries around the world. Documents such as parish registers, civil registration, land grants, deeds, probate records and wills, marriage bonds, funeral sermons, military rosters, guild membership lists, school attendance records, cemetery records, and passenger lists are all being copied. There are 1,800,000 rolls of microfilm in the library, and several thousand more are being added each month. Statistics are really not worth quoting because almost anything I tell you will be out of date when you read this. There are more than 200,000 printed volumes on the open shelves but 1,000 more are added each month. There are records of ten million families, and over 200 million names. A microfiche copy of the card catalogue showing the holdings of the library is available in all LDS family history centers across the country. You can be sure that wherever you live you will not be far from one. Microfilms can be ordered through a family history center and then viewed by you at the center.

If you want to look through the registers of the Evangelical Church of Hohenfriedeberg in Silesia (Schlesien); or of Grabau in Posen (Poznań); or Stallupönen in East Prussia (Ostpreussen); or get a list of everyone named Bernheim in the Evangelical church registers of Dortmund between 1710 and 1915; or information about Gerhard Eichler who was a goldsmith in Köln in 1785; or details of the next of kin who was a Feldwebel (sergeant) in the 18th Hussars in Vienna (Wien) in 1848— you can do all these things in your local family history center.

The International Genealogical Index™ (IGI) is based on names copied from church registers in many different countries and is subdivided into countries or areas making up a country during a period of history. For the Germanic area this means separating the records so that each of the old kingdoms and principalities or dukedoms is separately indexed. The German section contains more than a quarter of a million names. It includes baptisms or births, marriages, and deaths or burials. However, you must bear some things in mind before using the IGI:

1. It only includes names taken from the records that have been copied—very many church authorities will not cooperate with the LDS workers. In addition, the number of records to be copied is so great that in many areas less than 30 percent have, in fact, been copied. So always check whether the particular place in which you are interested is included in the IGI.

2. Copies are only as good as the person making the copy. Mistakes can be made, such as Wilhelm Müller being copied as Heinrich Müller. This is not so absurd as it sounds. One of my own ancestors appeared in the IGI for Lancashire, England as Thomas Caley, whereas the entry in the church register was Henry Caley. When I produced proof of the error the LDS records were corrected. There can also be omissions caused by the worker turning over two pages of a register together and thus missing a whole page of entries.

I don't mention these incidents as criticism of the work of the LDS Church, but only to point out the possibility of human error. Don't accept the IGI as the final word. It can be invaluable but is not infallible! If you don't find the name of your ancestor where you are sure it should be, then check the original church register.

The IGI was updated in 1993 and is available only on compact disc. It includes 14 million more names than the 1992 microfiche edition, as well as a number of enhanced features. The IGI is quite simple to use. The surname is on the left, followed in horizontal order across the page by the first name; the name of the wife or husband (if the entry is a marriage), or the names of the parents (if it is a baptism); the sex (M for a man, F for a woman); H for a husband, W for a wife; then the letter B for a birth or C for a christening, M for a marriage, N for a census, and W for a will. Finally, you arrive at the date of the event and the place.

Apart from the IGI, the most important LDS record is the Ancestral File™. This contains what are called family group sheets. They are submitted by church members and are the result of their own research. They are further divided into two sections—main and patrons. The main sheets have been checked for accuracy, the patrons have not. All the sheets from both sections give the same type of information as in the IGI, plus dates of death and burial of parents, and the names of the grandparents. All these records are also available on microfilm through the various LDS family history centers.

The 1993 update to Ancestral File is available on compact disc. Improved compression technology has permitted both the IGI and Ancestral File to contain millions more names on fewer discs. These compact disc editions have enhanced search and retrieval facilities and are altogether easier, quicker, and better to use than the previous microfiche editions.

Don't jump to conclusions about LDS records and say, "No member of our family has ever been a member of the LDS Church so there will be no point in checking the family group sheets." You may well have an unknown fourth or fifth cousin in the old country who is quite unknown to you. He or she may be a member of the LDS Church and may have traced the family back for many, many years.

In addition to the microfilms, the church has published many research papers containing genealogical information from many different countries. These can be bought (for a very small fee) through your local family history center or directly from the Family History Library in Salt Lake City. The booklets that contain information about the Germanic area of Europe have the following titles (the list is complete at the time of writing but may have been added to by the time you read this):

Major Genealogical Sources in Germany
Major Genealogical Sources in Switzerland
Major Genealogical Sources in the Netherlands*
Boundary Changes of the Former German Empire
Guide to Genealogical Sources in Austria
Guide to Genealogical Sources in Hungary
Austro-Hungarian Empire Boundary Changes
Church Records of the Netherlands**
The Origin of Names in the Netherlands
German Church Records
Hamburg Passenger List
Polish Research
Major Genealogical Sources in France
Major Genealogical Sources in Belgium
Major Genealogical Sources in Italy

If you are able to visit the library in Salt Lake City in person (more than 3,000 people do so every day), you will find more than 500 microfilm viewers available, and all the printed volumes are on open shelves. The parish registers are printed and indexed in alphabetical order.

The Family History Library does not do individual research, but it will answer specific questions. If you require detailed information, you will be mailed a list of researchers. When asking for this list be sure you specify your particular area of interest—you will then receive names and addresses of available researchers with knowledge of that area. At this point you make your own financial arrangements. However, bear in mind that you can do your own research on microfilm or microfiche in your nearest family history center, paying only a small fee for the purpose. So far as Germany is concerned, you may need a researcher's help

---

*There are also separate booklets for the various provinces of the Netherlands—Zeeland, Groningen, Friesland, Overijssel, Gelderland, North Holland, Utrecht, Limburg, North Brabant, South Holland, and Brenthe.

**There are also separate booklets for the various churches in the Netherlands—Dutch Reformed, Mennonites, Remonstrants, French Reformed, Evangelical Lutheran and Restored Lutheran, and Roman Catholic.

as you get further back in time because of the style of writing and the German script used in earlier documents.

One final word about LDS records so far as Germany is concerned. The German section of the IGI is rather curiously divided into four sections—Prussia, Germany, Saxony, and Hesse-Darmstadt. Don't be misled by these arbitrary divisions. I have found both Schleswig-Holstein and Silesia listed under Prussia. It is a little misleading to find the church registers of Skrave, in the former area under the heading of Prussia, side by side with the civil records of birth, marriage, and death of Lubsza, in Silesia. If you run into difficulty, be sure you check with the librarian of your local family history center.

JEWISH RECORDS

In all my previous books I have included a separate section on Jewish records and this book is no exception. This policy does cause me misgivings—why not separate sections on Lutherans and Catholics and Mennonites? Why not separate chapters for Saxons and Bavarians and Swabians? Do my Jewish readers object to being singled out in this way?

However, "Jewish" is not just another religion, nor is it a distinct nationality—but the Jews are a separate people. They are separated by centuries of persecution, of subjugation, of pogroms, of the diaspora, of genocide, and finally, the concentration camps of World War II. They must be treated separately—their genealogical problems are not the same as those of other groups, their vital records are not always the same records. Their areas of research are more limited, or conversely are more widespread. Their vital events are not always recorded, or if they are, they may often be found in the records of other denominations because their own were not legally recognized.

What records will you find of Jews expelled from England in the Middle Ages—their synagogues sacked, their personal property stripped from them before they sailed? What records will there be of a child who survived a day when the Cossacks put his village to the torch and the sword? What records survive from the ghettos of a thousand Jewish settlements in Eastern Europe? What records can be found when, as recently as the middle of the last century, a Jewish family might have no family name?

Sometimes such records will exist in the most unlikely of places—be it in New York or Vienna or Tel Aviv. Yes, the problems facing Jewish ancestor-hunters are profound—but not insurmountable. There are three factors that must remain uppermost in your mind at all times: the records you need are not necessarily to be found in Jewish archives; every year new sources of information are being discovered; and you will have problems with family names.

In the German-speaking areas of Europe, the Jewish people were subject to the same civil laws of the various states as were any other citizens, both up to the unification of Germany and since then. Civil registration started for the whole new country in 1875, but it had existed for many years before that date in several of the individual states. In many areas west of the Rhine it started in 1810, in Hannover in 1809, in Prussia in 1870, to quote just a few examples. Remember, too, that in many areas Jews could record the vital events of the family—births, marriages, and deaths—within their own community, but this had no legal basis. To protect property rights and the validity of wills it was necessary they be recorded in the church of the state religion—be it Lutheran or Catholic. Sometimes a child's first name registered in a church differed from that recorded in a synagogue.

Probably the greatest problem facing the Jewish ancestor-hunter is that of family names, and you should give a great deal of thought and attention to this subject before you become too deeply involved in your search. Often, names were simplified or anglicized—Kanofsky became Kane, Moses became Morris, Martinez became Martin, and so on. Another complication is the literal translation of a name, so that Zevi in Hebrew became Hart in English and Hirsch in German.

Because the Jewish people, in the main, lived in isolated settlements throughout Europe from the Middle Ages onwards, there was not the pressing need for a family name. "Moses, son of Aaron" was a sufficient description for recognition in a small, tightly knit community. In some cases—particularly among the Sephardim—family names based on occupations did develop in the 1600s, but they were frequently only used within the family and had no legal validity. It was not until the latter part of the eighteenth century that family names as we know them were in general use among European Jews.

In 1787 Austria ordered that all Jews should have family names; Frankfurt-am-Main followed in 1808; Napoleon enforced a similar law in the areas under his control in 1808, while Switzerland did not pass any law on the subject until 1863. When the Jewish people had to decide on a family name, their decisions were based on a wide variety of facts or fancies. Inevitably, the most popular ones were based on occupations or personal descriptions or locations—so a tailor became a Snider, a tanner a Leder (leather), a carpenter a Nagel (nail), a small man was Klein, a short one Kurtz, a religious and God-loving man was Gottlieb, a man from the east was Osterman. There were many other variations— in Frankfurt, houses were distinguished by signs instead of numbers, so very many Jews took names based on the sign on their house, and a Jew living in a house with the sign of a red shield became Rothschild, or Schiff if his house had the sign of a ship. In certain areas, such as the northwestern part of Germany, the name Rose was very popular for some unknown reason, and so in these districts there was a preponderance of names like Rose, Rosen, Rosenkrantz, Rosenbloom, Rosengarten, and so on.

Further complications are the use of patronymics (names based on that of the father)—Lewis-sohn, Aaronson, Abrahamson, Myerson—and on matronymics (names based on that of the mother)—Perle, Perlson, Gutkind, and so on. Patronymics and matronymics were used, too, in a more general way—in Slavic areas Wicz or Vitch were added to the father's or mother's first name, in Romania it would be Vici, in German areas Sohn or Witz.

For the above reasons it is often difficult to trace your Jewish ancestry back beyond the 1700s unless you have some family documentation to guide you. You may even find that after your ancestors had a recognized family name they changed it to that of a revered rabbi or a well-known Talmudic scholar.

So far as Jewish records in Europe are concerned, be sure you do not overlook the Hamburg Passenger Lists (see later in this book for full details), because this port and that of Bremen were the main places from which the emigrants from north and central Europe sailed to the New World. The Bremen records were destroyed by bombing in World War II, but the Hamburg lists exist from 1850 to 1934 (with the exception of Jan.–June 1853 and Aug. 1914–1919). The Bremen lists started in 1832 but were deliberately destroyed in 1874 because of lack of space. After that they were shredded every two years until 1907. From the latter date they were kept until their final destruction in 1944. There are a few copies in the State Archives in Koblenz (Karmeliterstrasse 1-3, 56068 Koblenz) which include 1907, 1908, 1913, and 1914. In addition, a list of emigrants who sailed from Bremen to New York is being compiled from U.S. sources by Gary J. Zimmerman and Marion Wolfert. Some 100,000 names for the period 1847–1867 have already been collected and published (see Bibliography).

If you already know the place from which your ancestors came, be sure you write to the local public library because many of the larger centers have Jewish collections containing a great deal of information about families in the area. These include detailed histories of Jewish communities. You will find that archivists and librarians are very helpful to Jewish inquirers from overseas. Try and overcome whatever deep-rooted feelings you may have and take advantage of these German sources—remember that most of the people you will be dealing with were born after the end of World War II.

The Weissensee Cemetery in Berlin is the largest Jewish cemetery in Europe. In the offices, there are over 115,000 index cards that give full details of each person buried there for over a century. You can obtain more details from Zentralarchiv der Juden in Deutschland, Fischerstrasse 49, 40477 Düsseldorf. Be sure you send two International Reply Coupons with your letter.

The Hamburg Jewish Cemetery—dating back to 1611—is located on Konigstrasse and is being restored. There are 7,000 graves here; about one-third are those of Sephardic Jews. The Hamburg Staatsarchiv has a register of the Jewish community in that city dating back to 1769.

The Berlin Document Center will continue to be administered by the U.S. Government until 1995. Its records include those of concentration camps, but access is limited to bona-fide historians. Further information can be obtained from the U.S. State Department.

Outside of Germany proper you will find Jewish records in other archives in what we call the Germanic area so far as language is concerned:

Austria

Jewish records are quite prolific for this country and are to be found in state archives, municipal offices, and magistrate's courts. For more information you should write to the Israelitische Kulturgemeinde, Bauernfeldstrasse 4, 1190 Vienna. For example, there are the records of 300 synagogues in the Burgenland area in the provincial archives (Landesarchiv Burgenland, Rusterstrasse 12-14, Freiheitsplatz 1, 7001 Eisenstadt). This area was part of Hungary until 1919 when it was ceded to Austria.

Hungary

There are a number of microfilms available of Jewish communities in the German-speaking areas of Hungary, and these are located in the National Archives of Hungary (Magyar Orzágos Levéltár, Bécsikapu tér 4, 1014 Budapest 1). Yad Vashem (see below) has a computerized list of half a million Hungarian victims of the Holocaust.

Poland

Some of the various regional archives have Jewish records from what were German-speaking areas, such as Bytom (Beuthen), Kraków, Gdańsk (Danzig), Legnica (Liegnitz), Opole (Oppeln), Posnań (Posen), Warszawa (Warsaw), Wrocław (Breslau), Zielona Góra (Grünberg). Many of these have been microfilmed by the Central Archives in Jerusalem. Yad Vashem has a computerized list of 204,000 residents of the Łódź ghetto, with dates of birth, death, and deportation. (See below for addresses for the Central Archives and Yad Vashem.)

ISRAEL

The organizations in Israel that hold records of various kinds from the Germanic area include:

The Central Archives for the History of the Jewish People
Givat Ram Campus, Hebrew University
Jerusalem 91010

The Jewish National and University Library
Givat Ram Campus, Hebrew University
Jerusalem 91010

Yad Vashem
Har Hazikaron, P.O. Box 3477
Jerusalem 91034

THE UNITED STATES

In the United States you will find almost all the records you will need in your research. Outside New York City there are the following organizations:

American Jewish Archives
3101 Clifton Avenue
Cincinnati, OH 45220

American Jewish Historical Society
2 Thornton Road
Waltham, MA 02154

In the city of New York there is the most magnificent assemblage of Jewish records anywhere in the world. I give below a very brief summary of the records held by the various organizations, but I make no claim to its completeness. You will find out more by writing directly and asking the particular source what information they have to solve your own particular problem. Be sure you cover return postage, and if you are helped, send a donation.

The Jewish Genealogical Society
P.O. Box 6398, New York, NY 10128
This organization numbers among its members all the leading Jewish genealogical experts. This enormous fount of knowledge is probably its greatest asset, but it also holds the Computerized Family Founder (CFF). This includes nearly 8,000 family names indexed alphabetically

in general, and within each community in particular, with details of those being actively researched at the moment. You may well be able to make contact with some unknown relative already researching your particular family.

Inquiries about the CFF should be addressed to the Jewish Genealogical Society, c/o Data Universal Corp., 1485 Teaneck Road, Teaneck, NJ 07666.

The Leo Baeck Institute
129 East 73rd Street, New York, NY 10021
The institute is mainly concerned with records from German-speaking areas. The library contains 50,000 volumes and 1,000 linear feet of archives. Areas well represented are Baden, Berlin, and West Prussia. There are also circumcision records from Aurich, Berlin, Filhene, Frankfurt-am-Main, Fürth, Munich (München), Randegg, Schildberg, Schleswig-Holstein, and Württemberg. There are marriage records from Berlin, Breslau, Dresden, and Nürnberg, and death records from Allersheim, Altstrelitz, Arnswalde, Berlin, Dyhernfurth, Frankfurt-am-Main, Gnesen, Haigerloch, Königsberg, and Potsdam. There are also some Memorbücher (yizkor books) and a number of family histories.

The YIVO Institute for Jewish Research
1048 Fifth Avenue, New York, NY 10028
In the main, the records here apply to the USSR and Poland rather than to Germany. However, it does have a collection of more than 500 Memorbücher, or yizkor books. These cover Jewish communities destroyed during World War II and in earlier pogroms. Most of them are in Hebrew or Yiddish and very few are indexed. Generally speaking, you will find that the books from Eastern Europe are based on the collective memories of survivors who met together and pooled their memories, whereas most of the German ones were written by individuals.

Aguadath Israel of America
5 Beekman Street, New York, NY 10038
Access to these Orthodox archives is by appointment only. There are a number of collections, including details of people rescued from Theresienstadt Concentration Camp, and minute books from youth groups in Fürth from 1919 to 1936.

Hebrew Union College (The Klau Library)
1 West 4th Street, New York, NY 10012
This organization holds many cemetery records from Graz (Austria), Frankfurt-am-Main, the Moselle area, Prague (Czech Republic), Vilnius (Lithuania), and Württemberg. It also has Memorbücher from Bavaria, the Nürnberg area, and Lvov (Lemberg).

The New York Public Library (Jewish Division)
Fifth Avenue at 42nd Street, New York, NY 10018

This has the largest collection of Judaica in the world, and the second largest collection of yizkor books in the city (second only to the YIVO Institute). It is impossible to list all the holdings, but the German collections include tombstone inscriptions from Köln, Nürnberg, Speyer, and Worms; genealogies from Germany and Lithuania; and records of many Jewish communities from the Germanic areas of Europe. You could happily and profitably spend two or three days here.

Research Foundation for Jewish Immigration
570 Seventh Avenue, New York, NY 10018

This organization has information on 25,000 individuals who emigrated from Austria, Germany, and the German-speaking areas of the former Czechoslovakia.

There are two other organizations in the city that may also be of value to you: The Bresky Library (3080 Broadway, New York, NY 10027) and the Mendel Gottesmann Library of Judaica and Hebraica and Archives (Yeshiva University Library, Amsterdam Avenue at 185th Street, New York, NY 10033).

CANADA

There is one Jewish genealogical society in Canada, located at the following address:

Jewish Genealogical Society of Canada
P.O. Box 446, Station A
Willowdale, Ontario M2N 5T1

Finally, do not be discouraged by your Jewish ancestral difficulties—bring to the search the tenacity, the patience, the determination, the intelligence, and the deep attachment to history of your ancestors.

ARCHIVES

Later in this book we will be talking about archives—those often mysterious places that hold many of the secrets of our ancestry. You will read about national archives, provincial archives, state archives, district archives, county archives, city archives, church archives, industrial archives, and even family archives. If you visit archives in person you will find they vary greatly—some are beautiful modern buildings, all glass and light, equipped with computers and microfilm readers, with charming, helpful archivists going out of their way to be helpful. Others look like something left over from the Middle Ages, with dusty shelves and even dustier books hidden away in dark corners and illuminated with 40-watt bulbs—presided over by unfriendly archivists who regard their treasures as their own personal property and you as an unwelcome visitor to be gotten rid of as quickly as possible.

It is impossible within the limited space of this book to list all the holdings of each individual archive, although I have done my best to cover all the main sources of information you will find. However, two of the many German archives must be discussed in some detail because (a) they are not widely known and may be overlooked, and (b) they have material of great value to people whose forebears came from some of the "lost territories" of Germany—Prussia (Ost und West Preussen), Silesia (Schlesien), Posen (Poznań), Pomerania (Pommern), the Sudetenland, Estonia (Estland), and Latvia (Lettland). The latter two countries also include areas that no longer exist as separate entities—Courland (Kurland) and Livländ (Livonia).

These two archives I mention are the Herder Institut in Marburg (Lahn) and the Evangelical Church Archives in Berlin.

The Johann-Gottfried-Herder-Institut
Gisonenweg 5-7, 35037 Marburg (Lahn)

As I mentioned earlier, German settlements were established in the Baltic area as early as the time of the Crusades. Over the years the

German areas in Estonia and Latvia were almost independent of the host countries. They maintained their language, their social customs, and their religion (mainly Protestant). In 1939 a treaty was signed between the German government and the two Baltic states, in which it was agreed that the records of the German settlements and churches could be filmed. Soon after the work began, the USSR took over the two countries, plus Lithuania, and incorporated them into the Soviet Union. However, the copying of the records continued until 1941. Lithuania was not included in the arrangements as the German areas in that country were practically nonexistent except for Memel. The Catholic church registers of that city and its suburbs are believed to be in the State Archives of Lithuania (Lietuvos valstybinis archyvas, 21 Kareiviu, Vilnius) and the Parish Register Archives (Lietuvos valstybinis metriku archyvas, 21 Kalinausko, Vilnius), while the registers of the Evangelical Reformed Church are in the Central Library of the Academy of Sciences (Lietuvos Moksly Akadem ijos Centriné Biblioteka, Vilnius).

In Estonia (Estland), a very large part of the material in the State Archives in Tallinn (Reval) and Tartu or Yurev (Dorpat) was copied. This material contains much information about the early German settlements in those areas, and includes records of the University of Dorpat; the city archives of Reval, including lists of citizens and property records; and records of the various craft guilds. The material was transferred to Berlin in 1941 and 1942, and a little later more than 700 rolls were sent to Posen (now Poznań, in Poland) where it was intended that a center for German-Baltic culture would be built after the war. In 1944 the records were transferred to Brunswick (Braunschweig) and came into the custody of the British army a year later. They were kept at Goslar until 1950 and were then transferred to the custody of the Baltic Historical Circle in Göttingen, and finally to the Herder Institut in 1952.

In Latvia (Lettland), nearly all the German records in the State Archives in Riga were filmed as well as those in the city archives. The latter included the registers of members of the various guilds, rolls of citizens from 1614 to 1812, rent books, land records and deeds, and a variety of other municipal records. From the areas of Latvia known as Courland and Livonia a number of "Seelenlisten" (church membership rolls) were also filmed, covering a period from the late eighteenth century until the middle of the nineteenth.

The films from Latvia reached the Herder Institut in the same roundabout way as those from Estonia.

Other miscellaneous records in the Institut include some family papers and family trees from Pomerania (Pommern), extracts from some church books (Kirchenbücher) from the same area—in particular from Schlawe from 1618 to 1710—and a few of these books from Silesia

(Schlesien). There are also the family and business papers of Gerhard Lange, from Schlawe, in which he mentions many individuals and families in that area during the last century. Finally, there is a small collection of biographies from the Sudetenland (now in the Czech Republic).

Many of the records are not in good condition. For a long period no funds were available to undertake repairs, but now some money has been made available and the work is going on. When you make inquiries of the Herder Institut, a small donation of a few dollars will be put to good use.

The films and manuscripts here, together with other items in the State Archives in Koblenz, form a unique collection of material for German-Baltic research. Some of the records in both locations have been filmed by the LDS Church. This filming is still continuing and it may be some time before the material is catalogued and available for public use. It consists mainly of Seelenlisten from Courland (Kurland) and Livonia (Livländ). The Acquisitions Division of the LDS library will be able to supply you with up-to-date information about this potentially valuable and continuing project.

Evangelisches Zentralarchiv in Berlin
Jebensstrasse 3, 10623 Berlin

One of the great adventure stories of genealogy is that of the successful removal of the great majority of the church registers (Kirchenbücher) of the Evangelical Church from the "lost territories" of Prussia, Posen, Pomerania, and Silesia in 1944 and their eventual safe haven in the central archives of the church in Berlin. These priceless treasures are not only of great value to ancestor-hunters, but also to Germans seeking to prove the dates of vital events in order to claim pensions and to obtain passports and inheritances. Almost all of the Kirchenbücher have been microfilmed by the LDS Church (which also played a large part in the preservation of the original registers).

The collection now in Berlin consists of more than 7,000 books from more than 500 different parishes in the territories mentioned above. There is no comprehensive index, but a number of the individual books were indexed by the ministers of the particular parishes. Sometimes this covers an extended period of several centuries, but often it only includes more recent entries. You can obtain detailed information about a parish from your nearest LDS family history center, or directly from Salt Lake City. The authorities at the Berlin archives will not undertake a detailed search but will answer a simple inquiry if return postage is covered—and I would add a personal note: send a small donation.

In the fall of 1944, when it became obvious that the area was in danger of invasion, the church authorities in the various centers—

Königsberg (now Kaliningrad), Danzig (Gdańsk), and Stettin (Szczecin)—ordered the ministers of the Evangelical churches to bring all records for shipment to the west in the area of Rhon (near Frankfurt). The great majority of the ministers complied and the books were stored in mine shafts. After the war the Kirchenbücher were damaged by thieves and arsonists, and many were destroyed. No list had been made of the books deposited, so it is not known which were stolen or destroyed and which were retained in the original churches. Since many of the latter are now under control of Russia and Poland, there is no certain information about the whereabouts of the missing Kirchenbücher. It is very fortunate that the books from the main centers such as Königsberg (with nineteen parishes) and Stettin (with twenty-two) are virtually complete. There are some records from Danzig but they are by no means complete. A number of the books there were handed over to the church authorities in 1943, but many ministers refused to surrender them when requested. There was a local dispute at the time because some believed the records would be used to discover which inhabitants were Aryan and which were non-Aryan. Most of the Kirchenbücher are believed to be now in the local Polish archives (Wojewódzkie Archiwum Państwowe, 80958 Gdańsk, Poland).

At the end of World War II, Paul Langheinrich, a member of the LDS Church, instituted a search for church books and records in the areas occupied by the Soviet forces. He was very successful in this effort and later obtained permission from the Soviet government to take all the books he had found to Berlin. The Red Army even provided a truck for this purpose.

At the same time, the LDS Church entered into negotiations with the Evangelical Church. The LDS officials explained they had no wish to retain the books when they discovered them, but only to copy them before returning them to the church. The Evangelical Church agreed to this and fully cooperated with the researchers of the LDS Church. At this time more Kirchenbücher were recovered from the areas I have mentioned and also from areas outside Prussia and Pomerania such as Posen and Silesia.

The Kirchenbücher available for Prussia and Pomerania are too numerous to list in this book, but there is space available to give details of the books from Silesia and Posen. Please bear in mind that the fact that a parish is mentioned does not mean that the records are complete, or that they cover a long period of time, so don't be too excited if you find the name of your ancestral town or village mentioned.

SILESIA (SCHLESIEN): Bunzlau, Goldberg, Grüssau, Hohenfrideberg, Karzem, Königszelt, Leopoldshain, Liegnitz, Marklissa, Reinersdorf, Rothenburg.

POSEN (POZNAŃ): Bromberg, Brostrowe-Friedheim, Cielle, Debenke, Fordon, Gogolin, Grabau, Gross Neudorf, Grünkirch, Krone-an-der-Brahe, Lobsens, Mrotschen, Nakel, Otterau-Langenau, Raschkow, Runowo, Sadke, Schulitz, Schweinert, Schwerin-an-der-Warthe, Sienno, Stenschewo, Weichselhorst, Weissenhöhe, Wilhelmsort, Wirsitz, Wissek, Zduny, Zinsdorf, Zirke.

Some Prussian records have now been transferred from Merseburg (Sachsen-Anhalt) to Berlin. They include property deeds. Although the records bear the title Prussian Cultural Heritage Secret State Archives, they are open for genealogical research.

Berlin Document Center

Control of this archive will be transferred from the United States to Germany in the near future. It contains the most comprehensive collection of Nazi files for 1933–45. The collection of thirty million documents includes the membership files of some ten million members of the Nazi Party, as well as personnel files of 600,000 Storm Troopers, 230,000 members of the S.S., and 60,000 S.S. officers.

Under the terms of the United States–Germany agreement all documents will be microfilmed before the transfer. The originals will be lodged in the Federal Archives in Koblenz—which already contains records of the Reichswehr (1919–35), the Wehrmacht (1935–45), and the German administrations in that part of Germany occupied by the Western allies. The original material in Germany and the microfilms in the United States will be open for public search.

THE LUTHERAN CHURCH

Since your German ancestors may have been members of the church in both the Germanic area of Europe and later in North America, you should be aware of changes that took place in 1986 in the organization of the church in both the United States and Canada. The various mergers that took place may change the locations of the church headquarters in both countries. This may also have an effect on the location of the church archives.

In the United States three Lutheran churches agreed to merge into a single church—the Evangelical Lutheran Church in America (ELCA), with national headquarters in Chicago. The three churches concerned were the Lutheran Church of America, the American Lutheran Church, and the Association of Evangelical Lutheran Churches. The Lutheran Church-Missouri Synod remains outside the new church because it is more conservative and does not practice open communion or allow women to be ordained as ministers. They are also more literal and conservative in their interpretation of the scriptures.

In Canada the three districts of the Lutheran Church in America acted jointly through the Lutheran Church in America—Canada Section. The Canadian counterpart of the American Lutheran Church has been independent since 1971 and was known as the Evangelical Lutheran Church in Canada (ELCC). The ELCC and the three synods of the Lutheran Church in America merged as of January 1, 1986 and are now called the Evangelical Lutheran Church in Canada (ELCIC). The church headquarters is in Winnipeg. There are a few other Lutheran groups in Canada which total about one percent of the Lutheran population.

The Missouri Lutheran Convention in August 1986 voted to give the Canadian districts of the church autonomy so that in future years there may be a separate branch of the Missouri Lutheran Church in Canada. The Missouri Lutheran districts in Canada are now known as the Lutheran Church—Canada.

THE GERMANS IN THE
UNITED STATES

Although the major period of German immigration into North America was in the nineteenth century, the first mass entry of German colonists was in 1683 when Germantown, in Pennsylvania, was founded. Even so, the description "mass" is a misnomer, since the party totaled thirteen families. However, it is easier to use the word "mass" to describe organized bodies of immigrants as opposed to the scattered entry of individuals or small family groups. It is quite possible that individual Germans landed before 1683, but we have no certain record of their arrival, although rumor has it that the earliest German settlers were in Virginia and Maryland as early as 1608.

From the early eighteenth century to the nineteenth century Germans settled in many states besides the three I have mentioned above—notably New York, the Carolinas, Texas, Wisconsin, Ohio, and Illinois. In this brief account of German immigration we must confine ourselves to major areas of settlement rather than attempting a complete history of all fifty states, or even those in the original thirteen colonies.

German settlement really commenced with the arrival of the "Palatines" in 1709 and their settlement in the colony of New York. Although the description "Palatine" really applied only to people from the Palatinate area of the Rhineland (now known as the state or land of Rheinland-Pfalz), it was also used to describe people from Baden, Bavaria (Bayern), Alsace (Elsass), Hesse (Hessen), and Württemberg.

There were a number of reasons for the great migrations—poor crops, bad winters, heavy taxes, military service, religious persecution and, most of all, the devastation caused by the Thirty Years War (1618–1648) and subsequent invasions of the Rhineland by France in 1673, 1688, and 1707. The winter of 1708–09 was the worst in Europe in more than a century. The intense cold started in October and continued until the end of April, and the vines and fruit trees in the southwest of the German area were destroyed. According to contemporary accounts, birds died in the air and spittle leaving the mouth was ice before it reached the ground. The disaster was total and the future without hope.

The Palatines started to arrive in London, England, via Rotterdam in 1708, and in 1709, according to some reports, 30,000 arrived between May and October. The refugees arriving in England had every intention of continuing their journey as soon as possible to Pennsylvania and the Carolinas. Representatives of these colonies had been active in the Rhineland proclaiming the attractions of good land and low taxes. William Penn himself paid several visits to the area, and in 1681 leaflets were distributed offering land in Pennsylvania at the price of two English pounds for 100 acres.

However, the English government, faced with a multitude of refugees beyond all expectations, blew hot and cold on the project. Objections were raised by English settlers already in the colonies and efforts were made to arrange settlement on various islands in the Caribbean, in England itself, and in Ireland. Meanwhile the Palatines continued to pour into London, and tented camps were set up in the suburbs, and houses, barns, and warehouses were requisitioned or donated.

Eventually some 3,000 Protestants were persuaded to settle in Ireland, where the policy of the English government was to dispossess the Catholic peasants and replace them with Protestants. By January 1710 more than 2,000 of the original 3,000 had settled in Co. Limerick and Co. Dublin, but another thousand had returned to London. Those remaining were given eight acres of land for every member of the family.

The great John Wesley, founder of the religious movement that bears his name, visited a Palatine community in Co. Limerick in 1760. He records in his journal: "I rode over to Killiheen, a German settlement, nearly twenty miles south of Limerick. In the evening I preached to another colony of Germans at Ballygarane. The third is at Court Mattrass, a mile from Killiheen. There is no cursing or swearing, no Sabbath-breaking, no drunkenness, no ale-house in any of them. How will these poor foreigners rise up in the judgement against those that are round about them." In spite of their difficulties, they survived, and there are many descendants in the area today with names like Switzer, Heck, Miller, and Shire.

Meanwhile, those left in London were living under very poor conditions—financial aid from the English government was minimal, but it was augmented by private donations obtained by the efforts of the Church of England. Inevitably, the refugees were accused of becoming a financial burden, of taking jobs away from the English, and even of introducing the plague into the country. Several of the camps and settlements were attacked by the London mobs and a number of Palatines were killed or wounded.

The leader of the first contingent to arrive in 1708 was the Rev. Joshua Kocherthal. His party consisted of forty-one people from Landau, in the Palatinate, and fourteen more from the same place joined them a few weeks later. It was eventually decided they should settle on the Hudson River, in the New York colony, some fifty miles north of New York City. They sailed in mid-October 1708 and took nine weeks on the voyage. Their settlement was named Newburgh.

By mid-summer of 1709 the Palatines were arriving at Rotterdam at the rate of a thousand a week. From there they were shipped to England in transport ships that had brought soldiers over to the Netherlands to fight in the War of the Spanish Succession. In September the English became worried about the number of Catholics among the refugees and some 3,000 were sent back to the Rhineland with a parting gift of five Dutch guilders.

In January 1710 the first mass sailing to the New World took place— some 600 Palatines left for the Carolinas and later founded the settlement of New Bern. In April 3,000 more sailed for New York. Eighteen hundred of them settled on the Hudson some ninety miles north of the city, while the balance stayed in the city itself. In 1712 the financial subsidies from the colonial government to the Hudson River settlers were abruptly ended. They were told they could hire themselves out as servants in New York or New Jersey but nowhere else. During the next five years many of them crossed into Pennsylvania, while others settled in Albany, Schenectady, and in Schoharie, on the Mohawk.

From 1717 onwards there was a steady stream of settlers into Pennsylvania, both from New York and directly from England. Many settlements were established in the eastern part of the colony between the Susquehanna and Delaware rivers and around the fast-growing city of Philadelphia. Pennsylvania was "the promised land" for the Germans— both those waiting in England and those now sailing directly from European ports. There were liberal terms for land purchase, religious toleration, and the existence of established German settlements and a way of life that made the colony irresistible.

Between 1727 and 1775 nearly 70,000 Germans went to Pennsylvania. A little earlier—in 1710—they had begun to enter Maryland in large numbers, and by 1756 the majority of the population was estimated to be of German origin. The main cause of this sudden departure from Pennsylvania was Indian attacks on the isolated German settlements and the refusal of the Quaker government to provide firearms for their protection. The main area of settlement was around Frederick and along the Monocacy River. At about the same time (1709–1729) small settlements were also established in Virginia and North Carolina. It is estimated that 200,000 Germans immigrated to North America in the eighteenth century and more than three million in the nineteenth. At the time of the Revolution nearly ten percent of the population was of German origin. In Pennsylvania German came close to being declared the official language.

Immigration tapered off towards the end of the eighteenth century because of industrialization in the German areas of Europe and consequent increased prosperity. There were also official restrictions on emigration in many of the states that were later to form the unified country of Germany, and an increase in compulsory military service. However, the pause was short-lived. By 1818 one bad harvest had followed another, the Napoleonic Wars had taken their toll of life and property, and religious disputes within the Lutheran Church had led to ill feeling and a disruption of orderly life. All these events led to another wave of emigration—this time from Bavaria (Bayern) and Württemberg, and later from Hesse (Hessen), Thuringia (Thüringen), and West Prussia (Westpreussen). By 1840 all the Germanic areas were contributing to the floodtide, but the majority still came from the southwest—mainly because of the history of close association with America and family connections with those already established in the great republic beyond the ocean.

The religious disputes I mentioned above were caused in the main by a compulsory union of the Reformed and Lutheran churches ordered by King Frederick William III of Prussia. A breakaway sect opposed to union and known as the "Old Lutherans" took the lead in the new emigration. More than a thousand went to the United States in 1839—700 to Wisconsin and the rest to Buffalo. In 1847 a large organized party left Lippe-Detmold in the North Rhineland for Missouri and Wisconsin, and in the following year more Missouri settlements were established by immigrants from Westphalia (Westfalen) and Hamburg. Smaller family groups went to the cities of Milwaukee and Cleveland.

At this time many Germans who were destitute had their passage overseas paid by their local community to save the increasing costs to the public purse. In the early 1840s a number of emigrant societies (generally known as Auswanderungsverein) were set up in various parts of the German area. They were organized on a cooperative self-help basis with the support of the various state governments. Their objectives were to help members to emigrate, and this help included both money and advice. The records of many of these societies—but by no means all—are in the state or city archives in Germany, together with copies of early newspapers devoted to the subject of emigration. The main centers were in the following places (the name of the existing state is given in parentheses):

Berlin
Breslau (now Wrocław, in Poland)
Darmstadt (Hessen)
Düsseldorf (Nordrhein-Westfalen)
Frankfurt-am-Main (Hessen)
Giessen (Hessen)
Hannover (Niedersachsen)
Karlsruhe (Baden-Württemberg)
Leipzig (Sachsen)
Mainz (Rheinland-Pfalz)
Stuttgart (Baden-Württemberg)

The high points in immigration into the United States in the nineteenth century were in 1854 when more than a quarter of a million Germans arrived, and in the period 1866–1873. The latter years saw the emergence of Prussia (Preussen) as the dominant state in the German area and a series of wars against Austria, Denmark, and France, culminating in the proclamation of the German Empire in 1870. In 1880 more than 200,000 Germans immigrated to North America. The estimates—and they can be no more than that—are that between 1820 and 1900 the number of immigrants totaled between three and five million.

Since those days there has been a steady flow of German immigrants, but not on the scale of the last century. The end of constant wars between the various states, the unification of Germany, and the end of cheap land in the United States all made the Fatherland a more attractive place in which to live, and this was reflected in smaller immigration figures. In 1900 the annual total was down to 20,000.

The main ports used by immigrants from Europe were New York, Philadelphia, Boston, Baltimore, and New Orleans. Some passenger lists for these ports do exist and you will find details later in this book. More information can be obtained from the National Archives in Washington and from the field branches in Anchorage, Atlanta, Boston, Chicago, Denver, Fort Worth, Kansas City, Los Angeles, New York, Philadelphia, San Francisco, and Seattle.

The ports used in Europe by emigrants consisted of several major ones and a number of small harbors such as Danzig (Gdańsk), Lübeck, Rostock, and Stettin. Practically no records exist of passengers leaving the smaller ports, but lists are available in various places for some of the main ports, and in most cases copies have been made by the LDS Church.

These ports are listed below with the location of the archives containing the records where they still exist:

Hamburg (1850–1934, except Jan.–June 1853 and Aug. 1914–1919), Museum für Hamburgische Geschichte, Holstenwall 24, 20355 Hamburg, Germany (for information contact Tourist Information am Hafen, Bei den St.-Pauli-Landungsbrücken 3, P.O. Box 102249, 20015 Hamburg)

Göteborg (1876–1913), Landsarkivet, P.O. Box 3009, Geijersgatan 1, 400 10 Göteborg, Sweden

Antwerp (1854 and 1855), Rijksarchief, Door Verstraeteplaats 2, 2000 Antwerp, Belgium

Le Havre (1749–1830), Archives Départmentale de la Seine-Maritime, 76100 Rouen, France

Bordeaux (1713–1787), Archives Départementale de Gironde, 33000 Bordeaux, France

Bremen records up to 1907 were destroyed by the authorities. Those since that date were destroyed by British bombing in World War II. Some lists of passengers bound from Bremen (1847–1862) have been compiled from U.S. sources and details are in the Bibliography.

It must be pointed out that the passenger lists in the various ports mentioned above have not all been indexed, and in order to obtain details it may be necessary to provide the name of the ship and the date of sailing. In some cases, indexing is now being done and you should check with the authority concerned for more detailed and up-to-date information.

When researching your ancestors in passenger lists you must always be on the lookout for name changes—misspellings, names written as they sounded, names simplified, names changed accidentally or deliberately by immigration officers, names that were anglicized, etc. Here are just a few examples taken at random:

Bekker	Baker	Roth	Ross
Brunn	Brown	Schmitt or Schmidt	Smith
Heinrich	Henry		
Hellmann	Hill	Schneeburger	Snow
Jong	Young	Stein	Stone
Konig	King	Wasser	Waters
Loewen	Lowe	Werfer	Weaver
Mann	Manning	Werner	Warner
Rickert	Richards		

Finally, while we are on the subject of names, remember diminutives (first names that are shortened) or "pet" names that bear little resemblance to the original. Here are a few examples:

Georg	Yuri, Jorg	Philip	Lipsi
Heinrich	Henni	Renate	Reni
Johann	Hansi	Rosina	Sina
Josef	Seppi	Rudolf	Dolf or Folph
Matthias	Tice	Wilhelm	Villie

As you are of German descent you should always remember that your ancestor may have settled in the United States after a brief stay in Canada, or he may have emigrated from the United States to Canada. Among many early Mennonite settlers there was a great deal of movement backwards and forwards across an unsupervised and unregulated border, and also many arranged marriages between a man settled in Ontario, Canada, and a woman in Pennsylvania or New York—or vice versa.

If you are not of Mennonite descent, then you may still come into cross-border problems because of the close friendship of Lutheran families in the two countries. An additional problem may possibly stem from a descent from one of the "Hessians"—the soldiers from the German area of Europe who fought in the British army during the American Revolution. The term "Hessian" is a misnomer. In fact, the German mercenaries came from many places in the Germanic area besides Hesse. They came from Brunswick, Anhalt-Zerbst, Anspach-Bayreuth, Prussia, Württemberg, and in fact from many other areas of Europe, including Austria, Estonia, Latvia, Hungary, and Italy.

After the United States became independent the German soldiers went their separate ways—some went back to their homes in Europe, some stayed in the United States, and many others crossed the border into Canada. Because of this general dispersal it has always been difficult to arrive at an estimate of their numbers, but it seems likely that at least 10,000 settled in Canada, where they were treated in the same way as the United Empire Loyalists and given grants of land in Nova Scotia, Québec, and Ontario. There is one story that in the period 1783–1793 they constituted ten percent of the marriageable male population of Québec; however, I find this high figure a little difficult to credit in view of the high birth rate of the Québecois and the population of the province at that time.

On their arrival in Canada they joined other German soldiers who had done their military service in Canada without crossing the border. The latter also qualified for the land grants. To further complicate matters, many of these "Canadian" Germans emigrated south to the United States a few years later, and others returned to Europe.

Virginia DeMarce, in her book *German Military Settlers in Canada After the American Revolution*, lists some 2,500 names. A few entries taken at random show the valuable genealogical information she has researched so painstakingly:

ABRAHAM, Daniel. Brunswick troops. Born Schorborn, aged 36 years 11 months, discharged in Canada 1783. Marysburgh, Ontario.

DUDLOFF, Gotlieb. Surgeon's mate. Regt. of Specht. Born Erichswalde, Saxony. Aged 28 years 7 months.

RAUCH, Joseph. Brunswick troops. Born Innsbruck. Aged 45. Discharged in Canada 1783.

SCHAEFFER, Andreas. Regiment de Barner. Born Kies, Wurzburg. Aged 29. Discharged Canada 1783.

SCHMIDT, Jacque. Private Corps Company. Hesse-Hanau Infantry. Discharged 1783. Born Bellersdorf. Aged 34.

There is more information to be found in the LDS Church records, in the National Archives of Canada in Ottawa, and in the provincial archives of the three provinces of Ontario, Nova Scotia, and Québec.

THE GERMANS IN CANADA

The number of German settlers in Canada was minute compared with the number in the United States, and settlement was confined to two provinces in the early days—Ontario and Nova Scotia. However, many of the Germans in Canada maintained close family and religious ties with German settlers in Pennsylvania and Maryland, and to discover more about your German ancestors in the United States you may find you need to do some of your research in Canada.

German settlers first entered the province of Ontario (then named Upper Canada) from Pennsylvania in about 1786, but there was no mass movement and during the next twenty-one years only twenty-five families settled in the southwestern area of the province—in what is now the city of Kitchener and the county of Waterloo. Many more followed in 1807 as land in Pennsylvania became too costly and frequent subdivision of farms within families reduced agricultural productivity. A German company was formed in Canada to promote immigration from Pennsylvania, primarily among Mennonites. An option was taken on 60,000 acres in 1803, and the purchase money of $40,000 was raised in the United States, mainly from Pennsylvania's Franklin County. A further 45,000 acres was bought a short time afterwards. In those early days all the Germans in Canada were related to families south of the border.

The settlers came from Franklin, Lancaster, Montgomery, and Bucks counties—particularly the townships of Bedminster, Hillborn, Plumstead, and Tinicum. Many of them were descended from Swiss-German Mennonites. The settlement area in Ontario was an isolated one beyond the districts officially opened by the government, and the Germans lived very self-contained lives. They shared a common language and customs and were bound together by the Mennonite religion. The steady influx from Pennsylvania ended by 1828 but was preceded in the early 1820s by a large number of arrivals—known as "Reichsdeutsche"—coming directly from Germany through the port of Halifax. The other source of

German settlement in scattered areas of Canada was that of the Hessians—mercenaries who had served with the British forces during the Revolutionary War. When the British were defeated and the United States created, the Hessians came north into Canada and received grants of land from the British government, mainly along the northern shores of Lake Ontario. However, the major and much more important settlement was in the southwest part of the province of Upper Canada and this we will talk about first, returning later to Nova Scotia.

The German area in Waterloo County was first known as Ebytown—named after an early Mennonite bishop, Benjamin Eby—and later as Sandhills and Berlin. The changes in immigration sources at this time—the early 1820s—led to important changes in the life of the area. The Mennonite farmers soon found themselves in a minority position as the later arrivals were primarily Lutheran and Moravian and were more interested in trade and manufacturing than they were in agriculture. By 1833 the words "Made in Berlin" on manufactured goods demonstrated the industrial growth of the area. It was true that good land could still be bought for two dollars an acre in the townships around Berlin such as Wilmot, Woolwich, and Wellesley, and there was still a steady drift north from Pennsylvania, but it was on a very small scale.

By the mid-1830s immigrants were coming to Berlin from all parts of the German area of Europe—Baden, Bayern (Bavaria), Hessen-Darmstadt, Elsass-Lothringen (Alsace-Lorraine), Holstein, Mecklenburg, Württemberg, and even from the German settlements in the Baltic areas of Estonia, Latvia, and Lithuania. No single religious group was predominant—by 1835 the Lutherans, Moravians, Baptists, and Swedenborgians had churches in the area, and by 1850 the Catholics. By this time more than 12,000 Germans had settled in Upper Canada.

In 1857 the Grand Trunk Railway had reached Berlin and the immigrants landing at Québec were able to travel directly to their destination by train. On one day in that year ninety German immigrants arrived in Berlin and thus increased the population by one percent in one day. Most of these newcomers were from Mecklenburg.

In 1916—in the middle of World War I—it was decided, as the result of a plebiscite, to change the name of Berlin to Kitchener. The new name was a tribute to the memory of a British general who had drowned earlier in the year when a battleship on which he was traveling had been torpedoed by a German submarine.

At the present time those of German descent in Kitchener, and in Waterloo County, are probably in a slight minority, but their influence in the area is strong and the history of the founding families is well documented. There are many instances where ancestor-hunters of Pennsylvania-German descent have found out more about their ancestry in

Kitchener than in Philadelphia or Harrisburg! There are a great many family histories, both published and in manuscript form, in the Grace Schmidt Room of the Kitchener Public Library and at Conrad Grebel College in the University of Waterloo. The latter has a large collection of Mennonite records, but not a great many church registers. It must always be remembered, of course, that the Mennonites practiced adult baptism, as did the Baptists.

There are many Mennonite sects in Ontario that do not deposit their records at the university, and you will have a difficult time in tracing their whereabouts. The Old Order Amish keep their genealogical records in the Amish Historical Library, RR4 Aylmer, Ontario N5H 2R3; but the following sects retain their records: Old Order Mennonite; Beachy Amish Mennonite; Old Colony Mennonite; Conservative Mennonite; Reformed Mennonite; Church of God in Christ, Mennonite; Evangelical Mennonite Mission; and Mennonite Brethren. However, most of the records of the original group of settlers from Pennsylvania are at the University of Waterloo.

Now let us turn to German settlement in the province of Nova Scotia. There is no connection between settlers there and those in Pennsylvania, except in a few isolated cases. The 3,000 Germans who settled in the province came directly from the German area of Europe, almost entirely by direct passage from the port of Rotterdam in the Netherlands to the port of Halifax, Nova Scotia. Settlement on an organized scale started in the mid-1700s when the British government was encouraging Protestant immigration into Canada. In the main, these Germans came from Baden, Hessen, Württemberg, and Rheinland-Pfalz, plus there were a few Swiss-Germans. Some twelve ships carried immigrants to Nova Scotia in the 1750s, and the passenger lists of ten of them have been researched and published by Terrence Punch, Nova Scotia's leading expert on German immigration into the province. Later in the century there was some settlement by the Hessian mercenaries whom I mentioned earlier.

The Germans in Nova Scotia settled mainly in the area of Lunenberg in 1753, but later moved into other places in this small province. There are a number of books about German settlement in Nova Scotia listed in the Bibliography.

RECORDS IN GERMANY

THE EVANGELICAL CHURCH

The Evangelical Church in Germany (Evangelische Kirche in Deutsch-land, E.K.D.) is a union of twenty-six largely independent territorial Lutheran, Reformed, and United churches (seventeen in the western part of the country and nine in what used to be East Germany). The two sections of the church are not yet officially unified but negotiations are taking place and already there is close cooperation. I list the addresses of the various church headquarters below. At the end of the list you will see the E.K.U.—this is a special association of United churches within the E.K.D. I also list three smaller communities that are affiliated with the E.K.D.:

Evangelische Landeskirche Anhalts
Kavalierstrasse 35, 06844 Dessau

Evangelische Landeskirche in Baden
Blumenstrasse 1, 76133 Karlsruhe

Evangelisch-Lutherische Kirche in Bayern
Meiserstrasse 11/13, 80333 Munich (München)

Evangelische Kirche in Berlin-Brandenburg
Neue Grünstrasse 19/22, 10179 Berlin

Evangelisch-lutherische Landeskirche in Braunschweig
Neuer Weg 88/90, 38305 Wolfenbüttel

Bremische Evangelische Kirche
Franziuseck 2/4, 28199 Bremen

Evangelisch-lutherische Landeskirche Hannovers
Rote Reihe 6, 30169 Hannover

Evangelische Kirche in Hessen und Nassau
Paulusplatz 1, 64285 Darmstadt

Evangelische Kirche von Kurhessen-Waldeck
Wilhelmshöher Allee 330, 34131 Kassel

Lippische Landeskirche
Leopoldstrasse 27, 32756 Detmold

Evangelisch-Lutherische Landeskirche Mecklenburgs
Münzstrasse 8, 19055 Schwerin

Nordelbische Evangelisch-Lutherische Kirche
Dänischestrasse 21/35, 24103 Kiel

Evangelisch-Lutherische Kirche in Oldenburg
Philosophenweg 1, 26121 Oldenburg

Evangelische Kirche der Pfalz
Domplatz 5, 67346 Speyer

Pommersche Evangelische Kirche
Bahnhofstrasse 35/36, 17489 Greifswald

Evangelisch-reformiete Kirche
Saarstrasse 6, 26789 Leer

Evangelische Kirche im Rheinland
Hans-Böckler Strasse 7, 40476 Düsseldorf

Evangelische Kirche der Kirchenprovinz Sachsen
Am Dom 2, 39104 Magdeburg

Evangelisch-Lutherische Landeskirche Sachsens
Lukasstrasse 6, 01069 Dresden

Evangelisch-Lutherische Landeskirche Schaumburg-Lippe
Herderstrasse 27, 31675 Bückeburg

Evangelische Kirche der schlesischen Oberlausitz
Schlaurother Strasse 11, 02827 Görlitz

Evangelisch-Lutherische Kirche in Thüringen
Dr. Moritz-Mitzenheim-Strasse 2a, 99817 Eisenach

Evangelische Kirche von Westfalen
Altstädter Kirchplatz 5, 33602 Bielefeld

Evangelische Landeskirche in Württemberg
Gänsheidestrasse 4, 70184 Stuttgart

Evangelische Kirche der Union (E.K.U.)
Herrenhauser Strasse 12, 30419 Hannover

Evangelische Brüder-Unität (Moravian Church)
Zittauerstrasse 24, 02747 Herrnhut (Oberlausitz)

Europäisch-Festlandische Brüder-Unität (Moravian Church)
Unitätshaus, 73087 Bad Boll

Bund Evangelisch-reformierter Kirchen (Federation of Reformed Churches)
Untere Karspüle 11a, 37073 Göttingen

Archiv und Bibliothek des Evangelisch Ministeriums (Archives)
Schmidtstedter 42, 99084 Erfurt

As you can see, in the past the Protestant churches in Germany were divided into several sects. If you know your emigrant ancestor from Germany was a member of the Evangelical Church, it will help you in your search if you can discover just which sect he belonged to in the old country.

You will find the various church headquarters staff anxious to be of help to you but you must not ask for the impossible. For example, people have been known to write to the North Elbian Evangelical Lutheran Church to the effect "My great-grandfather was a member of the Evangelical Church and came from somewhere near you. He was born in 1870 or thereabouts. Can you look up the baptism entry in the register?" The North Elbian area covers Schleswig-Holstein, Hamburg, Eutin, and Lübeck. You can imagine how impossible it would be to even start to search.

When you write to a church organization, or a small individual church, please remember to enclose an addressed airmail envelope and at least two International Reply Coupons. I am sorry to have to keep repeating myself on this subject, but if you do not pay the return postage you may not get a reply. In addition, it will not hurt your chances of successful cooperation if you offer, in advance, to pay whatever search fees are required. If the search is an easy one you may not be charged anything.

Finally, if you can, write in German. If you cannot, then at least end your letter with the words "Mit freundlichen Grüssen" ("With friendly greetings").

The headquarters of the Evangelical Church (E.K.D.) is:

Rat der Evangelischen Kirche in Deutschland
Jebensstrasse 3
10623 Berlin

German Lutheran Churches in Memel

When Memel was transferred to the USSR in 1945, the records of the Lutheran churches in the area disappeared from view. I have not been able to obtain any definite information about their present whereabouts, but it seems probable that they have been moved elsewhere, since several of the churches are now closed. The most likely present location is in the Lithuanian State Archives in Vilnius (see page 16).

The parishes concerned are Coadjuthen, Dawillan, Crottingen, Heydekrug, Kairinn, Karkelbeck, Kinten, Laugszargen, Nattkischken, Nidden, Paleiten, Paszieszen, Piktopen, Plaschken, Plicken, Prokuls, Ramutten, Rucken, Russ, Saugen, Schwarzort, Szugken, Wannagen, Wieszen, and Wischwill.

Evangelical Churches in East Prussia (Ostpreussen)

Before the invasion of East Prussia by the Red Army, the parish registers and church books (Kirchenbücher) from about 500 parishes were removed to what was then West Berlin. They are in the Central Archives of the Evangelical Church (Evangelisches Zentralarchiv in Berlin, Jebensstrasse 3, 10623 Berlin).

There are some missing and many gaps in the ones that survive, but if your ancestors came from East Prussia and were members of the Evangelical Church, these records may be vital to you. There is no listing of the parishes available, but the archives are planning a book about them.

Although 500 parishes are represented, there are in fact over 6,800 books involved, so you can see that the transfer and saving of these records was a major undertaking that reflects great credit on all the people concerned in this enterprise.

THE CATHOLIC CHURCH

The Catholic Church in Germany is organized in ecclesiastical provinces (each under an archbishop), bishoprics (Bistum), and the local parish (Pfarr). There are twenty-seven church archives. These hold the earlier parish registers, as well as confirmation and communion records and, in many cases, the Family Books (Liber de Statu Animarum). There is no countrywide accepted date for the surrender of early records to the various archives.

The Family Books were first introduced in 1614 and include full details of each family in the parish, together with the names of any servants, and the occupation of the head of the family. The books were kept in Latin and German and are more complete in some areas than in others. It was compulsory for the priest to maintain the books up to 1918, but since then it has been quite voluntary. The division of Germany after World War II did not affect the boundaries of the various dioceses, and so the re-unification in 1990 had no effect on ecclesiastical divisions.

The addresses of the various Catholic archives are set out below. It should not be difficult for you to decide to which address you should write. If, for example, your ancestors came from Wanzleben, a gazetteer or a good map in your local library will show you it is near Magdeburg, and the list below will give you the address for that diocese. Generally speaking, you will find that the headquarters of each Bistum is located in the largest city of the area:

AACHEN: Klosterplatz 7, 52062 Aachen
AUGSBURG: Fronhof 4, 86152 Augsburg
BAMBERG: Domplatz 3, 96049 Bamberg
BERLIN: Wundstrasse 48/50, 14057 Berlin
DRESDEN: Käthe-Kollwitz-Ufer 84, 01309 Dresden
EICHSTÄTT: Leonrodplatz 4, 85072 Eichstätt
ERFURT: Herrmannsplatz 9, 99084 Erfurt
ESSEN: Zwölfling 16, 45127 Essen
FREIBURG: Herrenstrasse 35, 79098 Freiburg
FULDA: Paulustor 5, 36037 Fulda
GÖRLITZ: Carl-von-Ossietzky-Strasse 41, 02826 Görlitz
HILDESHEIM: Domhof 18-21, 31134 Hildesheim
KÖLN: Marzellenstrasse 32, 50668 Köln
LIMBURG: Rossmarkt 8, 65549 Limburg
MAGDEBURG: Max-Josef-Metzger-Strasse 1, 39104 Magdeburg
MAINZ: Bischofsplatz 2, 55116 Mainz
MÜNCHEN: Rochusstrasse 5, 80333 München (Munich)
MÜNSTER: Domplatz 27, 48143 Münster
OSNABRÜCK: Hasestrasse 40a, 49074 Osnabrück
PADERBORN: Domplatz 3, 33098 Paderborn
PASSAU: Residenzplatz 8, 94032 Passau
REGENSBURG*: Niedermünstergasse 1, 93047 Regensburg
ROTTENBURG: Eugen-Boltz-Platz 1, 72108 Rottenburg
SCHWERIN: Lankower Strasse 14, 19057 Schwerin
SPEYER: Kleine Pfaffengasse 16, 67346 Speyer
TRIER: Hinter dem Dom 6, 54290 Trier
WÜRZBURG: Domerschulstrasse 2, 97070 Würzburg

Note: The national headquarters of the Catholic Church is Sekretariat der Deutschen Bischofskonferenz, Kaiserstrasse 163, 53773 Bonn.

The church registers are either in the original parish church or in one of the church archives listed above. Unfortunately, there is no hard-and-fast rule which says that registers must be sent to the archives on a certain date. In fact, there is no law at all controlling this matter. Even if a church is closed, it is not possible to say with certainty that the regis-

---

*A number of church registers from West Prussia are now in these archives. Detailed information is not available but if your Catholic ancestors came from a known location in West Prussia you should check whether the registers are here.

ters were then lodged in the church archives. They may have been transferred to the nearest church remaining in operation.

If you know the exact location of the place from which your ancestor came, you can probably identify the particular archive that may have the registers. If you cannot, then I would write to the Sekretariat and ask them where the registers for that particular church are now.

OTHER CHURCH GROUPS

The two largest of the Protestant free churches, the Methodists and the Evangelical Community (Evangelische-Gemeinschaft), joined in 1968 to form the Evangelical Methodist Church (Evangelisch-Methodistische Kirche). There is also the Alliance of Free Evangelical Congregations—Baptists (Bund Evangelisch-Freikirchlicher—Baptisten), as well as Mennonites, Quakers, and Jews. By and large, all these organizations leave the registers and other records in the individual churches.

In 1933 there were over half a million Jews living in Germany. Today there are thirty thousand in the former Federal Republic and about seventy Jewish congregations—the largest being in what was West Berlin and in Frankfurt-am-Main with over five thousand members each. Figures are not available for the former D.D.R. The address for the Jewish headquarters is:

Zentralrat der Juden in Deutschland
Fischerstrasse 49
40477 Düsseldorf

THE CALENDAR

Before searching German records, you should be aware of changes in the calendar which, over a period of some years, produced either opposing and contradictory systems, or two different systems existing side by side.

Until 1582 the Julian calendar, established by Julius Caesar, was used in Germany and, indeed, in all civilized countries. This calendar divided the year into 365 days, plus an extra day every fourth year. The system was in operation until 1582, but astronomers had discovered that it exceeded the solar year by eleven minutes—or three days every four hundred years. Between the date when the Julian calendar was established in 325 and the year 1582, the difference amounted to eleven days. Since this affected the calculations for Easter, Pope Gregory XIII decreed that ten days be dropped from the calendar in order to bring Easter to the correct date. To prevent a recurrence of the problem, he also ordered that in every four hundred years leap year's extra day be omitted in a centennial year when the first two digits could not be divided by four without a remainder.

Are you still with me? Well, it means that it was omitted in 1700, 1800, and 1900 but will not be omitted in 2000. The Pope also changed the beginning of the New Year from March 25 to January 1, and this new system became known as the Gregorian calendar.

Generally speaking, the new calendar came into force in Germany between 1582 and 1585, depending on the locality. There were some places that started it later and the most important of these are listed below:

Prussia (Preussen)	1612
Pfalz-Neuburg	1615
Osnabrück	1624
Minden	1630
Hildesheim	1631
Friesland	1700

Basically, the Protestant areas were reluctant to make the change, while the Catholic areas started as soon as possible after the papal decree was issued. So you will find places where the Catholic Church accepted the New Year as starting on January 1 and so called September the ninth month, while the Lutheran Church in the same place regarded March 25 as the New Year and regarded September as the seventh month.

When the change did take place, it led to confusing entries of dates in church registers for a brief period. Once the reason is clear to you, you will not be puzzled to find that an ancestress of yours had one child born in one year and a second born a few months later. It was the calendar that changed and not the nine-month gestation period, so all is well!

CHURCH RECORDS

Some church records date back to the fifteenth century, but in fact you should not expect to find many of them before about 1563 for the Catholic Church and a few years later for the Lutherans. Some of the exceptions are to be found in Baden and Württemberg, where there are Lutheran registers dating back to 1531 and 1545 respectively.

Although civil registration did not come into force until recent times, very early church registers often contained detailed information about individuals in the parish. Remember, of course, that most church records showed only dates of baptism, marriage, and burial, and you may never find out the dates of birth and death.

Many of the registers have been destroyed as the result of civil wars, rebellions, and invasions over the centuries, but in some cases duplicates were kept in a separate location, so all is not necessarily lost. In Mecklenburg, for example, copies were kept from 1740 onwards.

If you are searching church registers in person, you must be prepared to cope with entries in Latin (until the mid-nineteenth century) and the old German script, plus bad handwriting, and even a style of handwriting that is very different from that of the present day. No one ever said ancestor-hunting was easy!

Illegitimacy was fairly common in some rural areas of Germany. The illegitimate children were always baptized, but often the entry was made upside-down or sideways to emphasize the difference. The entry itself was very specific. The child was a bastard (Hurenkind), the mother a whore (Hure), and the father a fornicator (Hurer) or an adulterer (Ehebrecher).

The entries in the church registers usually include the following information:

BAPTISMS: Name, sex, date, names of parents, father's occupation, place of birth, names and addresses of godparents.

MARRIAGES: Name, age, and address of bride and bridegroom, occupation of groom, names and addresses of parents, occupation of the two fathers.

BURIALS: Name, age, place of death, cause of death, names of parents, name of husband or wife if still alive, date and place of burial.

Usually the above entries were made in three separate registers, but occasionally you will find all three events entered in one register in chronological order as they occurred.

In some parishes, particularly in the eighteenth and nineteenth centuries, you may find Family Books (Familienbücher or Liber de Statu Animarum). These contained complete records of a family and are of great genealogical value. Always check in a particular locality with the Catholic priest or the Lutheran minister as to the existence of a Family Book.

The book showed the name of the head of the household at the time the entry was made, the full names of the various members of the household, their places of birth, their marital status, the dates of death of deceased family members, and the place to which a family member moved if he or she left home (for marriage, work, or emigration). Check also for Kirchenbuchduplikate, a duplicate of entries in the church register which was sent each year to the nearest headquarters of the particular church.

OTHER CHURCH RECORDS

Grave Registers (Grabregister)

These were maintained in the parish church, and although they were a duplicate of the entry of burial in the church register, they often contained additional information such as the date of death and the exact age (i.e., 38 years, 204 days). As the burial entries usually gave the date of *burial* and the age only in years, the grave registers can be of great help.

Church Receipt Books (Einnahmebücher)

These gave details of payments received from church members for such services as bell-tolling for a funeral (with name of deceased and date), and payment for burial plots and funeral cloths (Leichenhemden).

Confirmation Records (Konfirmationbücher)

Most children were between thirteen and twenty when they were confirmed, in both the Catholic and the Lutheran churches. The list gives the child's name and place and date of birth; the name and occupation of the father; and—quite often—the later marriage of the child. These records are either in the original churches or in the church archives.

There is one problem you should consider in connection with church records. If you know the religion of your ancestor but have problems with the location of his or her birthplace because you discover a number of places in Germany with the same name, you may find some help in knowing which religion was predominant in certain areas.

For example, let us suppose you know your Catholic ancestor came from a place named Schwarzenberg. You find there is one place with that name in Hesse (Hessen), one in Brandenburg, one in Prussia (Preussen), and one in Bavaria (Bayern). The odds are that the place you want is in Bavaria, because Brandenburg and Prussia are mainly Lutheran, and Hesse is Protestant but not necessarily Lutheran. This is not an infallible method, but it may help.

The other problem that may cause you difficulty, particularly in Schleswig-Holstein and Friesland, is different naming practices. Farms carried a name, usually the one given to them by the original owner.

The name stayed with the farm even when the ownership changed. The trouble is that when a new owner bought the farm he would take its name as his own or, if a man's wife inherited a farm, he would change his name to her maiden name. This could produce the complication of children bearing different surnames within the same family. If you run into this problem, find out if the confirmation books are available for the particular parish, because these records usually give the original name and the later one.

Another naming problem makes life even more difficult. If you see Wilhelm Brode von Magdeburg, for example, in a list, it does not necessarily mean that Wilhelm was a noble. It could simply be that he was a man named Wilhelm Brode who came from Magdeburg. It could be the case that he had moved from Magdeburg to Hannover and found that Brode was a common name, and so to distinguish himself from all the other Wilhelm Brodes he added the words "von Magdeburg." A generation later it could be shortened by his son to Ernst von Magdeburg.

So the surname may, in fact, be your guide to the actual place of origin of the family. Your next problem will be to discover the original surname, and this you may find if you can trace the baptismal or confirmation record of Ernst, because they are likely to give the true surname.

The final naming problem in this particular area is that of the practice of using patronymics—the naming of a child by giving him a new surname based on the first name of the father. Thus Wilhelm, son of Ernst Borgman, could be christened as Wilhelm Ernst. In instances like this, you must again have recourse to baptismal and confirmation records in order to trace the real surname. If you trace an ancestor back to a particular place and find no one of that name in the place before him, then your most obvious reaction is to assume he must have come there from elsewhere. However, do not make this assumption until you have checked out the possibility of a name change.

PASSENGER LISTS

In most countries these are either nonexistent or so few in relation to the whole that they need not be considered as a source of genealogical information. In Germany, however, the story is very different, and that is why I put them second to church registers as a good source of information. In fact, they are equally vital to people whose ancestors came from many other countries in Europe—Austria, Bulgaria, the former Czechoslovakia, Hungary, Poland, Romania, Serbia, the Scandinavian countries, and the former USSR.

Bremen and Hamburg were the main ports for European emigration from 1832 (Bremen) and 1845 (Hamburg) up to 1934. Unfortunately, the Bremen lists were destroyed, but the Hamburg lists are available and on microfilm. They contain the names of over five million people who emigrated through the port and microfilm copies of the lists are located in the Historic Emigration Office (Museum für Hamburgische Geschichte, Holstenwall 24, 20355 Hamburg; for information write c/o Tourist Information am Hafen, Bei den St.-Pauli-Landungsbrücken 3, P.O. Box 102249, 20015 Hamburg). If you know the exact year of emigration, the cost of a search will be at least thirty dollars per name and year searched. For this you will receive an official certificate, which will include the information that appears in the original passenger list: passenger's name, age, occupation, hometown, date of departure, and sometimes his marital status, number of children, and destination.

On the other hand, the LDS Church has also microfilmed the lists, and I think you will find it cheaper to deal with them (35 North West Temple, Salt Lake City, UT 84150).

The State Archives in Hamburg house the original passenger lists of emigrants who sailed overseas directly from Hamburg, or indirectly via Hamburg to other European ports. For example, many emigrants sailed to a British port such as Gravesend or Harwich, crossed the country by train, and then sailed overseas from Liverpool. The period covered by the passenger lists is from 1850 to 1934, with the exception of January to June 1853 and August 1914 to 1919. However, the lists were only compiled for ships with more than twenty-five passengers. They are indexed on a yearly basis in rough alphabetical order. The LDS index is more accurate.

The passenger lists are divided into direct and indirect records. Most emigrants traveled *directly* to a port in their new homeland. For example, the great majority of emigrants to the United States landed in New York; from there they scattered across the country and to Canada and South America.

You will not need to search the lists, of course, if you already know the place of origin of your emigrating ancestor, and the details of his or her family. It will be much easier and less expensive to try other sources first (family stories, diaries, Bibles, naturalization records, or letters).

It is important to realize that not all emigrating Germans used Hamburg or Bremen. Some sailed from Le Havre in France. You must remember, too, that the place of origin shown in the passenger lists is not always the birthplace. However, in that case the odds are that the place of birth was quite near the place of domicile. For example, your ancestor may be shown as coming from Herrenhäusen (a small city), whereas his place of birth may have been Neuburg, a little village a few miles away.

Even if you find no record in the Hamburg lists, all is not lost. Several of the German states kept their own records of emigration from the state, notably Brunswick (Braunschweig), Hesse (Hessen), and Württemberg. Other similar records were kept in many individual cities and towns.

If you are consulting the lists yourself the following glossary may be of help to you:

Alter	Age
Anschrift	Address
Auswanderer	Emigrant
Beruf	Occupation
Bestimmungsort	Destination
Datum	Date
Erwachsen	Adult
Geboren	Born
Geburtsort	Birthplace
Gewerbe	Occupation
Herkunftsort	Place of origin
Kinder	Children
Länder	Provinces or states
Ledig	Single
Namen	Names
Nationalität	Nationality
Ort	Place
Strasse	Street
Verheiratet	Married
Vorname	Given name
Wohin	Destination
Zuname	Surname

Other possible sources of information are the official lists of permits to emigrate. Most of these have been lost, but some have been published for the areas of Brunswick (Braunschweig), Nassau, Sachsen-Weimar, and Waldeck. The German Genealogical Society of America has copies of these.

Another source of information about arrivals in the United States from the Germanic areas of Europe is a series of volumes called *Germans to America: Lists of Passengers Arriving at U.S. Ports 1850–1891*, ed. Ira A. Glazier and P. William Filby. This is an on-going project.

Names

In your search of records remember it was common in the middle 1700s in the Germanic areas to use only the *second* baptismal name in official records in later life. The first name was that of a parent or grandparent and was given as a compliment but never used officially. So Oskar Georg Weber would only appear as Georg Weber.

OFFICIAL RECORDS

Civil Registration (Reichspersonenstandsgesetz)

This started in 1875 following the unification of Germany, but only so far as the main Germanic area was concerned. In some areas the system had started earlier. There is a Register Office (Standesamt) for each particular area. All records of births, marriages, and deaths are kept there, but a duplicate of each entry is sent to the state capital. It should be noted that a registration area can be quite large, covering several towns and villages.

In those areas originally under French control, such as Alsace-Lorraine (Elsass-Lothringen) and a few other small areas west of the Rhine, registration started in 1810; in Frankfurt (once a Free City) it began in 1850, in Lübeck and Oldenburg in 1811, in Hanover (Hannover) in 1809, and in most parts of Prussia (Preussen) in about 1870. The death registers are particularly useful because they very often give not only the place and date of death, but also the names of the parents of the deceased and any surviving children.

Wills (Testamente)

The probate system in Germany is a little complicated. Once a lawyer has drawn up a will, a copy is deposited in the district courthouse (Amtsgericht) for the area in which the testator is *living*. The local authorities then notify the Civil Register Office (Standesamt) in the district where the testator was *born*. When he dies, the Standesamt in his place of death notifies the Standesamt in his place of birth, and the latter, in turn, notifies the Court of Law of the location of the will. The court then executes the will. Original wills are either in the district courthouse or in the state archives (Staatsarchiv) in each province.

Censuses (Volkszählungen)

These have been held on a countrywide basis since 1871, but others were held at irregular intervals in various areas. Germany has traditionally conducted the censuses through the states, or provinces, rather than through the central government:

GERMANY: 1871, 1880, 1885, 1890, 1895, 1900, 1905, 1910, 1919, 1925, 1933, 1939

WEST GERMANY: 1946, 1950, 1961, 1970

EAST GERMANY: 1946, 1964

BADEN: 1852, 1855, 1858, 1861, 1867, 1925, 1933, 1946

BADEN-WÜRTTEMBERG: 1946, 1950, 1961, 1970

BAYERN (BAVARIA): 1846, 1849, 1852, 1855, 1858, 1861, 1867, 1946, 1950, 1961, 1970

BERLIN (WEST): 1945, 1946, 1950, 1961, 1970

BERLIN (EAST): 1945, 1946, 1964

BREMEN: 1900, 1905, 1946, 1950, 1961, 1970

DRESDEN: 1871

HAMBURG: 1866, 1867, 1871, 1946, 1950, 1961, 1970

HESSEN (HESSE): 1925, 1946, 1950, 1961, 1970

KÖLN (COLOGNE): 1961

NORDRHEIN-WESTFALEN (NORTH RHINE-WESTPHALIA): 1946, 1950, 1961, 1970

PREUSSEN (PRUSSIA): 1895, 1900, 1905, 1910

RHEINLAND-PFALZ (RHINELAND-PALATINATE): 1946, 1950, 1961, 1970

SAARLAND: 1927, 1935, 1961, 1970 (see under France for 1945–57)

SCHLESWIG-HOLSTEIN: 1803, 1835, 1840, 1855, 1860, 1946, 1950, 1961, 1970

WÜRTTEMBERG: 1821, 1832, 1843, 1846, 1849, 1852, 1855, 1858, 1861, 1867, 1946, 1950

DEUTSCHER ZOLLVEREIN: 1855 (This was the area included in a Customs Union of North German States.)

Many of the above census returns have been copied by the LDS Church.

The federal government receives the results from the states in order to make a "national head count," but the original returns are kept in the individual states and copies can be obtained from the municipal archives (Stadtarchiv) or the Civil Register Office (Standesamt) in each city or district. East Germany, when it was independent, destroyed its census returns after counting.

In order to consult the census returns or obtain a copy of the original return, you will, of course, need to have an address in either a city or a village. For the former you will want a street name but for the latter it is not so essential. When writing, you should give the full name of your ancestor, if known, and the names of his or her spouse and children. This will enable the authorities to distinguish between people of the same name. It will be no use asking for a copy of the census return of Wilhelm Müller in Neudorf, Hessen; there might be twenty of them living there at the same time. Wilhelm Erich Müller would narrow it down, and Wilhelm Erich and his wife, Elisabeth, and his sons, Erich and Heinrich, would pinpoint it.

You must also be prepared to find that some census returns were destroyed by bombing in the Second World War. It may be wise for you to contact the central census authority and ask if the census returns exist for a particular location and where they are located. The address is:

Statistisches Bundesamt
Gustav Stresemann Ring 11
Postfach 5528
65189 Wiesbaden

In addition to the censuses listed above there were others conducted at irregular intervals over the years by individual cities, for example, Mecklenburg in 1819. You will have to check on these by writing to the state and municipal archives for the area in which you are interested.

Police Registration (Einwohnermelderegister)

This started in most of the states in about 1840 and controlled internal movement. The records included full name, family details, date and place of birth, and occupation. As I mentioned earlier in this chapter, the records are usually held in local archives, police headquarters, or state archives.

Military Records (Kriegslisten)

These are incomplete and not always easily accessible but they are worth working on because every male was liable for military service in the various state armies. If your ancestors came from the Schleswig-Holstein area, you are luckier than most. The system there involved the registration of every male child at birth, and the record was kept up to date as far as addresses were concerned until his call-up date. A good sequence of discoveries can follow: if you find your ancestor's addresses from the military records, you can trace the census returns; if you find the census returns you find the place of birth; if you find the place of birth you find the church records, you lucky people from Schleswig-Holstein! The military lists in general date back to the early 1700s and are in the state archives.

Certificate of Birth (Geburtszeugnis or Geburtsbrief)

When a person wanted to establish citizenship in a city or town, or get married, or join a guild (see overleaf), he or she would have to produce this document. The individual had to produce a letter from the priest or pastor in his or her birthplace and the civil authorities would then issue the certificate.

Guild Records (Gilderbücher)

These can provide valuable information for you. The guild (like the trade union of today) was powerful in the work field. It permitted its members to work only at a particular trade, in a particular place. It made sure that a newcomer in town became a citizen before he joined the guild. Remember that being an inhabitant was not the same as being a citizen. Anyone could be an inhabitant, but you had to earn the right to become a citizen. You had to work hard, not be a charge on the community, not be a bastard, be sober, be a churchgoer, and know the right people.

Then, and only then, the good citizen could apply to join a guild, and the guild records show his name, his trade, the names of his wife and children, the date and place of his birth, the date and place of his marriage, and the date of his arrival in the city and his entry into the guild. The guilds exercised so much control over their members that they could dictate the area of the city in which they lived, and even whom they married (preferably the daughter of another guild member).

The guild records are either in local archives or in state archives, and they date back in many cases to the early seventeenth century, and in a few instances even earlier.

Other Available Records

There are three important sources of information in Germany that are often overlooked. They are, in order of value, Ortssippenbücher (Local Family Books), Geschlechterbücher (Lineage Books), and Leichenpredigten (Funeral Sermons).

These records should be used in conjunction with all the other sources I have listed; none of them, on their own, will provide you with all the answers, but they may well fill gaps, solve relationship puzzles, and give you the place of origin, marriage, or death of a particular ancestor. Unfortunately, the records I mention are not in any one place, nor are the locations listed. You will have to write to the particular place or general area in which you are interested: to the Mayor (Bürgermeister) for a village, town, or city; or to the local Catholic priest or Lutheran minister; or to the director of the city archives (Stadtsarchiv) or the provincial archives (Landesarchiv or Staatsarchiv). You will have to ferret out the locations for yourself, but I never promised you a Rosengarten!

One final word of warning: be sure to send two International Reply

Coupons and a self-addressed airmail envelope, and be prepared for a little resistance in some places to producing the Ortssippenbücher for reasons made clear below.

Local Family Books (Ortssippenbücher)

German genealogists and sociologists have been very interested since the early part of this century in studying the various families living in a particular area. This is partly pure research, partly love of history, and partly the German passion for tidiness, for having everything in its proper place. The Ortssippenbuch for a particular area will list all the members of every family (living and dead) and their relationship with each other. The source of the information was, of course, the church register, both Lutheran and Catholic.

As interest in the projects grew, the organization of them was taken over by a branch of the government, and as each district was completed, the results were published in book form. The ultimate aim was to have a genealogical record of the entire German people.

This was a point where the interests of genealogists in tracing family descent coincided with the National Socialist racial policies for a brief period. After 1933 many German citizens, particularly farmers, store-owners, and teachers, were required to provide a certificate proving their Aryan descent—der Ahnennachweis, as it was called—and the existence of a completed Ortssippenbuch for their district simplified their task. The tracing of lineage was required back to the early nineteenth century; only the S.S. demanded lineage back to 1750 for their members.

Publication was suspended in 1940; after the war the task was taken over by the genealogical organizations without regard to any racial purity, and today some 150 books are in print. In addition, very many books were started and never finished, or finished and never printed. You will find the books or manuscripts in local and state archives. The present-day compiling of the books is not being done on a very even basis, since it depends very much on the energy and dedication of the various genealogical organizations. About half of the completed books refer to districts in the Länder of Baden and Hessen-Nassau.

It should be mentioned that some manuscripts are still in the possession of the individuals who worked on them, and if you are referred to a private individual, your approach should be a tactful one, since not everyone wishes to be reminded of the original reasons for their genealogical research.

German Lineage Books (Deutsche Geschlechterbücher)

These books date back in some cases to the late eighteenth century when the first known one was published. The contents, of course, go back very much further. They contain the details of descent of bourgeois families, i.e. middle class and lower upper class, not the nobility. Each book contains a number of family trees of various German families. They are on a regional basis in that all the families in the book are from one district.

Some 200 of the Geschlechterbücher have been published, and more are on the way. Each family section starts with the earliest known member and descends through the years to the date of publication. It also lists occupations, and places of baptism, marriage, death, and residence.

Funeral Sermons (Leichenpredigten)

This source of genealogical information is almost unique to Germany but I have found similar records in Hungary. They originated in the sixteenth century for a rather odd reason. When the Reformation reached Germany it meant the end of a very ornate and impressive funeral mass in the Catholic Church. This was a great occasion in which the deceased was praised at length by a local orator (often a professional, paid for his services), a large choir performed, and a sermon was delivered by the local priest (or by the bishop if the dead man or woman was important enough, or if the remaining spouse was generous to the church).

The end of this kind of ceremony left a gap in the lives of many people, mainly among Lutherans and Calvinists. They had embraced a simple and stark religion, but many of them missed a good funeral mass! So the funeral sermon was born and took the form of a eulogy at the graveside. Some sermons were entirely religious in content, but many were biographical and recounted the whole life of the deceased with details of births, marriages, public or military service, and other events of note.

After the ceremony the sermons were printed and circulated to all the friends of the family. There are well over 100,000 of these preserved in various locations and covering the period from about 1550 up to around 1800. Some of them are only a page or two in length, but some, if the deceased was famous, run to a hundred pages or more!

You can usually depend on the information contained in them being accurate; since the sermon was to be circulated among family and friends there was no point in lying or exaggerating the life and accomplishments of the deceased. Obviously, certain events would probably be quietly ignored: a period of insanity, a bastard child, dishonorable discharge from the army, a conviction for theft—that sort of thing would be left unsaid.

You can see that these three sources may well be of great value to you. Remember, though, that two of them are limited in their scope. The Lineage Books are confined to the bourgeois families, the Funeral

Sermons to the wealthier Protestants, and only the local Family Books record everybody, Catholic and Lutheran, rich and poor, in fact all classes of society.

Because the records I have mentioned are scattered in so many municipal offices, libraries, and archives, the search for one that includes your own family may be long-drawn-out, but if you are successful you may find your family lineage for a good many years, even two or three centuries.

There are still more available records of use to you. In some localities you will find all of them, in others only one or two:

	Approximate starting date
Adressbuch (City Directory)	1750*
Bürgerbuch (Citizenship Record)	1300
Familienregister (Family Registers)	1800
Gerichtsprotokolle (Court Records)	1500*
Grundbücher (Land Records)	1000*
Lehrlingsbücher (Apprentice Records)	1550
Polizeiregister (Police Registers)	1800
Stadtchroniken (City Chronicles)	1600
Steuerbücher (Tax Records)	1400
Zeitungen (Newspapers)	1800*

The dates are approximate because they vary from province to province, and from city to city. Generally speaking, the records marked with an asterisk are in the provincial archives (Staats- und Landesarchiv) and the others in city archives (Stadtarchiv) or district archives (Kreisarchiv), but there are exceptions to this.

One of the major problems about German records of interest to the ancestor-hunter is that they are scattered among church archives, state archives, city, town, and village archives, some government departments and offices, libraries, and museums. To make matters worse, only one attempt has been made to list the location of all genealogical archives and that effort, though praiseworthy, is very incomplete. Make no mistake: the material is there; it is available and informative; and it goes back over the centuries. Even minor local events were recorded and will be of interest to you.

ARCHIVES

The many divisions of the Germanic area are the cause of the peculiar distribution of archives. From the fourteenth to the nineteenth century, central power over the Germanic lands was exercised by the Hapsburg dynasty, so the central archives of the old Reich are in Vienna (Wien).

Since then, the various states have preserved their own archives; as a result, there are archives of all kinds scattered throughout both Germanys, from major cities down to small villages, and there are no central archives with precious genealogical records.

You will find Staatsarchiv (national), Staatsarchiv (provincial), Landesarchiv (provincial), Stadt (city), Bezirk (district), Dorf (village), Familien (family), Dom (cathedral), Pfarr (parish), Gutsarchiv (property), plus many others for individuals, families, professions, manufacturing plants, religious orders, and youth organizations.

In the following pages you will find details of many of the archives of value to the ancestor-hunter: first, the provincial or state archives; then a list of local archives alphabetically by city, town, and village; finally a list of church archives at a level lower than those included earlier in this chapter. In addition you will find a list of archives devoted to the papers of noble families.

State Archives (Staatsarchiv)

BADEN-WÜRTTEMBERG:
Hauptstaatsarchiv
Konrad-Adenauer Strasse 4
70173 Stuttgart

BAYERN:
Hauptstaatsarchiv
Arcisstrasse 12
80333 Munich 2

BERLIN:
Staatsarchiv
Archivstrasse 12-14
14195 Berlin

BRANDENBURG:
Landeshauptarchiv
Sanssouci, Orangerie
14469 Potsdam

BREMEN:
Staatsarchiv
Präsident Kennedy Platz 2
28203 Bremen

HAMBURG:
Staatsarchiv
ABC Strasse 19
20354 Hamburg

HESSEN:
Hauptstaatsarchiv
Mainzerstrasse 80
65189 Wiesbaden

MECKLENBURG-VORPOMMERN:	Hauptarchiv Graf Schack Allee 19053 Schwerin
NIEDERSACHSEN:	Hauptstaatsarchiv Planckstrasse 2 30169 Hannover
NORDRHEIN-WESTFALEN:	Hauptstaatsarchiv Prinz Georg Strasse 78 40479 Düsseldorf
RHEINLAND-PFALZ:	Staatsarchiv Karmeliterstrasse 1-3 56068 Koblenz
SAARLAND:	Landesarchiv Am Ludwigsplatz 7 66117 Saarbrücken
SACHSEN:	Hauptarchiv Archivstrasse 14 01097 Dresden
SACHSEN-ANHALT:	Hauptarchiv Hegelstrasse 25 39104 Magdeburg
SCHLESWIG-HOLSTEIN:	Landesarchiv Schloss Gottorf 24837 Schleswig
THÜRINGEN:	Hauptarchiv Marstallstrasse 2 99423 Weimar

City Archives (Stadtarchiv)

The type of record you will find in local archives includes all or some of the following. It is up to you to write and find out what is available for your particular district. Try to write in German, because even though there may be someone there who understands English, he or she may not read it well enough to understand just what you want to know. I once wrote and asked for the correct name of a book about leading families in a particular city. I had a reply in flawless English telling me they had only one copy of the book, and in any case it would be too heavy to send through the mail! They did not mention the name of the book, either, so I had to write again in German, and then all was well.

You may also find that when you write in English you will be answered in German. In this case you can try to find someone who speaks German, a friend or a local teacher, or settle down with a good German-English dictionary in the local library.

At this point let me again remind you to enclose a self-addressed airmail envelope and two International Reply Coupons to cover return postage. If you are planning a great deal of correspondence with Germany, it will save money if you buy German stamps. Write to the post office (Postamt) of any German city, enclose a bank draft for a sum of money (five or ten dollars), and ask them to mail you German stamps of the right value for airmail letters to this country.

The type of records you will find are listed below:

Address Books (Adressbücher)
Apprentice Lists (Lehrlingsbücher)
Census Returns (Volkszählungen)
City Chronicles (Stadtchroniken)
City Directories (Adressbücher)
Citizenship Lists (Bürgerbücher)
Court Records (Gerichtsprotokolle)
Emigration Lists (Auswanderungregister)
Family Books (Ortssippenbücher)
Family Registers (Familienregister)
Funeral Sermons (Leichenpredigten)
Grave Registers (Grabregister)
Guild Books (Gilderbücher)
Land Records (Grundbücher)
Lineage Books (Geschlechterbücher)
Newspapers (Zeitungen)
Parish Registers (Kirchenbücher)
Police Registers (Polizeiregister)
Probate Records (Testamente)
Tax Records (Steuerbücher)
Wills (Testamente)

The following abbreviations are used in the list of cities, towns, etc., to show the provinces or Länder in which the places are located:

BW   Baden-Württemberg
B   Bayern
BL   Bremen
BR   Brandenburg
H   Hessen
HL   Hamburg
MV   Mecklenburg-Vorpommern

NS   Niedersachsen
NW   Nordrhein-Westfalen
RP   Rheinland-Pfalz
S   Saarland
SA   Sachsen
SAA Sachsen-Anhalt
SH   Schleswig-Holstein
T   Thüringen

Aachen (NW)
Aalen (BW)
Abensberg (B)
Ahaus (NW)
Ahrweiler (RP)
Alsfeld (H)
Altdorf (B)
Altena (NW)
Altenburg (SA)
Alt-Wallmoden (NS)
Alzey (RP)
Amlishagen (BW)
Amöneburg (H)
Amstetten (B)
Andernach (RP)
Anklam (MV)
Annaberg-Buckholz
  (SA)
Annweiler (RP)
Ansbach (B)
Apolda (T)
Arnsberg (NW)
Arnstadt (T)
Artern (SAA)
Aschaffenburg (B)
Ascherleben (T)
Aue (SA)
Augsburg (B)
Babenhausen (H)
Bacharach (RP)
Backnang (BW)
Balingen (BW)
Bamberg (B)
Baunatal (H)

Bayreuth (B)
Beeskow (BR)
Bensheim (H)
Bentheim (NS)
Bergisch-Gladbach
  (NW)
Bad Bergzabern (RP)
Berleburg (NW)
Berlin
Bernburg (SAA)
Besighem (BW)
Bevensen (NS)
Biberach (BW)
Bielefeld (NW)
Bingen (RP)
Bischofswerda (SA)
Bitterfeld (SAA)
Blaubeuren (BW)
Blomberg (NW)
Bocholt (NW)
Bochum (NW)
Bonn (NW)
Borken (NW)
Borna (SA)
Bottrop (NW)
Flecken Bovenden
  (NS)
Brafkenheim (BW)
Brakel (NW)
Brandenburg an der
  Havel (BR)
Brandestein bei Elm
  (H)
Braunschweig (NS)

Breckerfeld (NW)
Breisach (BW)
Bremen (BL)
Bremerhaven (BL)
Brilon (NW)
Brühl (NW)
Bad Buchau (BW)
Bühl (BW)
Büren (NW)
Burg auf Fehmarn
  (SH)
Burg bei Magdeburg
  (SAA)
Burgbernheime (B)
Burghausen (B)
Burgkunstadt (B)
Burgsteinfurt (NW)
Burkheim am K
  (BW)
Butzbach (H)
Buxtehude (NS)
Calbe (SAA)
Calw (BW)
Castrop-Rauxel
  (NW)
Celle (NS)
Cham (B)
Chemnitz (SA)
Coburg (B)
Coesfeld (NW)
Coswig (SAA)
Cottbus (BR)
Crimmitschau (SA)
Cuxhaven (NS)

Darmstadt (H)
Deggendorf (B)
Deidesheim (RP)
Delitzch (SA)
Demmin (BR)
Dessau (SAA)
Detmold (NW)
Diez (RP)
Dillingen/Donau (B)
Dingolfing (B)
Dinkelsbühl (B)
Dinslaken (NW)
Doberlug-Kirchhain
    (BR)
Donauwörth (B)
Dornburg/Elbe
    (SAA)
Dorsten (NW)
Dortmund (NW)
Dreieichenhain (H)
Dresden (SA)
Dubeln (SA)
Duderstadt (NS)
Duisburg (NW)
Dulmen (NW)
Düren (NW)
Bad Durkheim (RP)
Düsseldorf (NW)
Eberbach (BW)
Eberswalde (BR)
Ebingen (BW)
Eckernförde (SH)
Edenkoben (RP)
Eggenfelden (B)
Eichstatt (B)
Eilenburg (SA)
Einbeck (NS)
Eisenach (T)
Eisenberg (RP)
Eisenberg (T)
Eisfeld (T)
Eisleben (SAA)
Ellwangen (BW)

Emden (NS)
Emmerich (NW)
Bad Ems (RP)
Endingen (BW)
Engen (BW)
Erding (B)
Erfurt (T)
Erkelenz (NW)
Erlangen (B)
Eschwege (H)
Esslingen/Neckar
    (BW)
Eutin (SH)
Feuchtwangen (B)
Flensburg (SH)
Forchheim (B)
Forst/Lausitz (BR)
Bad Frankenhausen
    (SAA)
Frankenthal (RP)
Frankfurt/Main (H)
Frankfurt/Oder (BR)
Frechen (NW)
Freiberg (SA)
Freiburg/Breisgau
    (BW)
Freising (B)
Freudenstadt (BW)
Friedberg/Hessen (H)
Friedrichshafen
    (BW)
Fritzlar (H)
Fulda (H)
Furstenau (NS)
Furstenwalde (BR)
Fürth (B)
Füssen (B)
Gaildorf (BW)
Gardelegen (SAA)
Garmisch/
    Partenkirchen (B)
Geinhausen (H)
Geislingen (BW)

Gelsenkirchen (NW)
Gengenbach (BW)
Gera (T)
Gernrode (SAA)
Gerolzhofen (B)
Geseke (NW)
Gevelsberg (NW)
Giengen (BW)
Giessen (H)
Glücksburg (SH)
Glückstadt (SH)
Gnandstein (SA)
Göppingen (BW)
Görlitz (SA)
Goslar (NS)
Gotha (T)
Göttingen (NS)
Greifswald (MV)
Greiz (T)
Greussen (T)
Grimma (SA)
Groitzscg (SA)
Grossbottwar (BW)
Gross-Gerau (B)
Grünberg (H)
Grunstadt (RP)
Guben (BR)
Gudensberg (H)
Güstrow (MV)
Hachenburg (RP)
Hagen (NW)
Halberstadt (SAA)
Halle an der Saale
    (SAA)
Hamburg (HL)
Hameln (NS)
Hanau (H)
Hann/Munden (NS)
Hannover (NS)
Haslach (BW)
Hattingen (NW)
Heidelberg (BW)

Heidenheim/Brenz (BW)
Heilbad Heiligenstadt (T)
Helmstedt (NS)
Herberg/Elster (BR)
Herford (NW)
Herne (NW)
Herrenberg (BW)
Hersbruck (B)
Bad Hersfeld (H)
Herten (NW)
Hildburghausen (T)
Hilden (NW)
Hildesheim (NS)
Hochstadt (B)
Hof (B)
Hofgeismar (B)
Homberg (H)
Bad Homberg (H)
Horb/Neckar (BW)
Hornburg (NS)
Höxter (NW)
Hüfingen (BW)
Husum (SH)
Ilmenau (T)
Ingelheim (RP)
Ingoldstadt (B)
Iserlohn (NW)
Isny (BW)
Itzehoe (SH)
Jena (T)
Jever (NS)
Jülich (NW)
Juterbog (BR)
Kaiserlautern (RP)
Kalkar (NW)
Kamenz (SA)
Kandel (RP)
Karlshafen (H)
Karlsruhe (BW)
Karlstadt (B)
Kassel (H)
Kaufbeuren (B)

Kelheim (B)
Kempen (NW)
Kempten/Aligäu (B)
Kenzingen (BW)
Kiel (SH)
Kirchheim/Teck (BW)
Kirn (RP)
Kirtorf (H)
Kitzingen (B)
Kleve (NW)
Koblenz (RP)
Köln (NW)
Königshofen (B)
Konstanz (BW)
Korbach/Edersee (H)
Köthen/Anhalt (SAA)
Kranenburg (NW)
Krefeld (NW)
Bad Kreuznach (RP)
Kronach (B)
Krönberg (H)
Kulmbach (B)
Kusel (RP)
Lage-Lippe (NW)
Lahnstein (RP)
Lahr (BW)
Landau (RP)
Landsberg (B)
Landshut (B)
Bad Langensalza (T)
Laubach (H)
Lauenburg/Elbe (SH)
Lauf (B)
Laufen (B)
Lauingen/Donau (B)
Lauterbach (H)
Lauterecken (RP)
Leipzig (SA)
Lemgo (NW)
Leutkirch (BW)
Leverkusen (NW)
Lich (H)

Lichtenfels (B)
Limburg/Lahn (H)
Lindau (B)
Linz (RP)
Lippstadt (NW)
Löbau (SA)
Lörrach (BW)
Lubben (BR)
Lübeck (SH)
Luckenwalde (BR)
Lüdenscheid (NW)
Ludwigsburg (BW)
Ludwigshafen (RP)
Ludwigslust (MV)
Lügde (NW)
Lüneburg (NS)
Lünen (NW)
Magdeburg (SAA)
Mainz (RP)
Mannheim (BW)
Marburg (H)
Marienberg (SA)
Markdorf (BW)
Markleeberg (SA)
Marktredwitz (B)
Marl (NW)
Maulbronn (BW)
Mayen (RP)
Meckenheim (NW)
Meersburg (BW)
Meiningen (T)
Meisenheim (RP)
Meissen (SA)
Meldorf (SH)
Melle (NS)
Memmingen (B)
Menden (NW)
Mengen (BW)
Meppen (NS)
Bad Mergentheim (BW)
Merseburg (SAA)
Messkirch (BW)
Metelen (NW)

Mettmann (NW)
Meuselwitz (SA)
Michelstadt (H)
Mindelheim (B)
Minden (NW)
Mittweida (SA)
Moers (NW)
Möhringen (BW)
Mönchengladbach
 (NW)
Monschau (NW)
Montabour (RP)
Mühldorf (B)
Mühlhausen/Thur (T)
München (B)
Münnerstadt (B)
Münster (NW)
Bad Münstereifel
 (NW)
Namedy (RP)
Nassau (RP)
Nauheim (H)
Naumburg/Saale
 (SAA)
Neckarsteinach (H)
Neheim/Hüsten
 (NW)
Neuburg (B)
Neuenburg (BW)
Neuenhaus (NS)
Neumünster (SH)
Neuötting (B)
Neuss (NW)
Neustadt (B)
Neustadt/Donau (B)
Nidda (H)
Nideggen (NW)
Nordhausen (T)
Nordhorn (NS)
Nordlingen (B)
Northeim (NS)
Nürnberg (B)
Nürtingen (BW)
Oberhausen (NW)

Obernburg/Main (B)
Oberndorf (BW)
Oberursel/Taunas
 (H)
Oberviechtach (B)
Ochsenfurt (B)
Oelsnitz im Vogtland
 (SA)
Offenbach/Main (H)
Offenburg (BW)
Ohrdruf (T)
Ohringen (BW)
Oldenburg (SH)
Oldenburg (NS)
Bad Oldesloe (SH)
Olpe (NW)
Opladen (NW)
Oppenheim (RP)
Oranienburg (BR)
Oschatz (SA)
Oschersleben (SAA)
Osnabrück (NS)
Osterburg (SAA)
Osterrode/Harz (NS)
Otterberg (RP)
Otterndorf (NS)
Paderborn (NW)
Paschim (MV)
Pegau (SA)
Perleberg (MV)
Pforzheim (BW)
Pfullendorf (BW)
Pfullingen (BW)
Pirna (SA)
Plauen im Vogtland
 (SA)
Porz (NW)
Pössneck (T)
Prenzlau (MV)
Pritzwalk (BR)
Bad Pyrmont (NS)
Quakenbrück (NS)
Quedlinnburg (SAA)
Radolfzell (BW)

Rain (B)
Rastatt (BW)
Ratingen (NW)
Ratzeburg (SH)
Ravensburg (BW)
Rees (NW)
Regensburg (B)
Reichenbach im
 Vogtland (SA)
Reinheim (H)
Remagen (RP)
Remscheid (MW)
Rendsburg (SH)
Reutlingen (BW)
Rheda/Wiedenbrück
 (NW)
Rheinberg (NW)
Rheine (NW)
Rhein Hausen (NW)
Rheydt (NW)
Rhoden (H)
Riedlingen (BW)
Rieneck (B)
Riesa (SA)
Rinteln (NS)
Rochlitz (SA)
Romrod (H)
Rosberg (NW)
Rosenheim (B)
Rostock (MV)
Rotenburg (NS)
Roth (B)
Rothernburg (B)
Rottweil (BW)
Rudolstadt (T)
Ruhla (T)
Rüthen (NW)
Saalfeld (T)
Saarbrücken (S)
Saarlouis (S)
St. Goar (RP)
St. Ingbert (S)
Salzgitter (NS)
Bad Salzuflen (NW)

Bad Salzungen (T)
Salzwedel (SAA)
Sangerhausen (SAA)
Schalkau (SAA)
Schleiz (T)
Schleswig (SH)
Schleusingen (T)
Schlitz (H)
Schmalkalden (T)
Schmölin (SA)
Schneeberg (SA)
Schönebeck (SAA)
Schongau (B)
Schopfheim (BW)
Schorndorf (BW)
Schotten (H)
Schramberg (BW)
Schwabach (B)
Schwäbisch Gmünd
   (BW)
Schwäbisch Hall
   (BW)
Schweinfurt (B)
Schwelm (NW)
Schwerin (MV)
Schwetzingen (BW)
Seefeld (B)
Seehausen/Altmark
   (SAA)
Seligenstadt (H)
Sendenhorst (NW)
Senftenberg (BR)
Siegburg (NW)
Siegen (NW)
Sigmaringen (BW)
Sindelfingen (BW)
Singen (BW)
Sinsheim (BW)
Sondershausen (T)
Sonneberg (T)
Bad Sooden (H)
Speyer (RP)
Sprendlingen (H)
Stade (NS)

Stadthagen (NS)
Stassfurt (SAA)
Stendal (SAA)
Stockach (BW)
Stockum (NW)
Straelen (NW)
Stralsund (MV)
Straubing (B)
Stuttgart (BW)
Suhl (T)
Sulz/Neckar (BW)
Tangermunde (SAA)
Telgte (NW)
Tittmoning (B)
Bad Tolz (B)
Torgau (SA)
Traunstein (B)
Treffurt (T)
Trier (RP)
Tübingen (BW)
Überlingen (BW)
Uelzen (NS)
Ulm (BW)
Ulrichstein (H)
Unna (NW)
Velbert (NW)
Verden/Aller (NS)
Viersen (NW)
Villingen (BW)
Vohburg/Donau (B)
Volklingen (S)
Wachtenheim (RP)
Waiblingen (BW)
Bad Waldsee (BW)
Waldheim (SA)
Waldshut (BW)
Wangen (BW)
Wanne-Eickel (NW)
Warendorf (NW)
Warstein (NW)
Wasserburg am Inn
   (B)
Wattenscheid (NW)

Weiden-Oberpfalz
   (B)
Weil am Rhein (BW)
Weilburg (H)
Weilheim (B)
Weimar (T)
Weingarten (BW)
Weinheim (BW)
Weismain (B)
Weissenburg (B)
Weissenfels (SAA)
Werl (NW)
Werne an der Lippe
   (NW)
Wernigerode (SAA)
Wertheim (BW)
Wesel (NW)
Wetzlar (H)
Wiesbaden (H)
Wilster (SH)
Bad Wimpfen (BW)
Bad Windsheim (B)
Winsen (S)
Wismar (MV)
Witten (NW)
Wolfach (BW)
Wolfenbüttel (NS)
Wolgast (MV)
Wolmirstedt (SAA)
Wormeln (NW)
Worms (RP)
Wülfrath (NW)
Wünsiedel (B)
Wuppertal (NW)
Würzburg (B)
Xanten (NW)
Zeitz (SAA)
Zella-Mehlis (T)
Zerbst (SAA)
Zeulenroda (T)
Zittau (SA)
Zweibrücken (RP)
Zwickau (SA)

I do not claim that the above list is complete. It has been put together from a variety of sources, and there will probably be omissions, particularly of smaller places. Correspondence should be sent to the Direktor, Stadtarchiv, followed by the name of the city and the province or Länder.

In addition to the above, there are specialized archives in such places as Jena, for example, where you will find the archives of the Karl Zeiss Company and the Jena Glassworks. If you know your ancestor worked for a large corporation it may be worthwhile to write to the company concerned to ask if it has archival or personnel records available.

There is also the Red Cross Archives in Dresden (Das Zentral Verwaltungsarchiv des Deutschen Roten Kreuzes, Kaitzerstrasse, 01069 Dresden). This may be useful if you are trying to trace someone who was a refugee from the area of Germany now in former Soviet territory.

Parish Archives (Pfarrarchiv)

Many of the city archives shown above also have local church records, but given below are separate church archives known to exist and *not* included in the major church archives previously listed. After the province code, a C or L is given in parentheses to indicate whether the archives hold Catholic or Lutheran records, or both.

Amöneburg (H) (C)
Balingen (BW) (L)
Biberach (BW) (L and C)
Bochum (NW) (L)
Bottrop (NW) (C)
Brakel (NW) (C)
Burgsteinfurt (NW) (L and C)
Duderstadt (NS) (L and C)
Duisburg (NW) (L)
Dulmen (NW) (L)
Emden (NS) (L)
Emmerich (NW) (L and C)
Engelskirchen (NW) (C)
Erfurt (T) (L and C)
Essen (H) (C)
Flensburg (SH) (C)
Göttingen (NS) (L and C)
Gudow (SH) (L)
Hagen (NW) (L and C)
Hattingen (NW) (L)
Herford (NW) (L and C)
Herrenberg (BW) (L)
Hof (B) (L)
Höxter (NW) (C)

Isny (BW) (L)
Karlsruhe (BW) (L)
Kassel (H) (L)
Kulmbach (B) (C)
Leer (H) (L)
Lich (H) (L)
Lübeck (SH) (L)
Methler (NW) (L)
Molzen (NS) (L)
Munstereifel (NW) (L)
Neuss (NW) (L)
Remagen (RP) (L and C)
Rottweil (BW) (C)
St. Goar (RP) (L)
Schwäbisch Hall (BW) (L)
Siegburg (NW) (C)
Stockum (NW) (C)
Überlingen (BW) (C)
Uelzen (NS) (L)
Viersen (NW) (C)
Wattenscheid (NW) (L and C)
Wetzlar (H) (L and C)
Xanten (NW) (C)
Zweibrücken (RP) (L)

Family Archives (Familienarchiv)

Many of the princely, noble, or prominent German families have either donated their family papers and records to the state or opened their documents to the general public. Searches can be made without charge, or by a fee, according to local decision. These family archives may be located in the original family residence (usually a Schloss, or castle) or in archives in the state, the city, or the village. You will have to do some letter-writing about this because the variations are infinite. If your ancestors were employed by these families, or were tenant farmers on the estate, the information can be of very great value to you.

The family archives I have been able to discover are listed below, showing the place, the abbreviation for the province or Länder, and the name of the family. (*Note*: The province codes are the same as those used above.)

Adelebsen (NS), Adelebsen
Ahausen (NW), Spee
Alme (NW), Spee zu Alme
Altenhof (SH), Reventlow
Althausen (BW), Württemberg
Amecke (NW), Wrede-Amecke
Amorbach (B), Leiningen
Anholt (NW), Salm
Antfeld (NW), Papen zu
    Antfeld
Apelern (NS), Münchhausen
Artelshofen (B), Harlach
Aschhausen (BW), Zeppelin
Assenheim (H), Solms-
    Rödelheim
Assumstadt (BW), Waldburg-
    Wolfegg
Aufsess (B), Aufsess
Augsburg (B), Fugger
Aulendorf (BW), Königsegg-
    Aulendorf
Banteln (NS), Benningsen
Beetzendorf (SAA), Von der
    Schulenburg
Beichlingen (T), Werthern-
    Beichlingen
Bentlage (NW), Wittgenstein-
    Berleburg

Berleburg (NW), Wittgenstein-
    Berleburg
Besselich (RP), Barton-Stedman
Bietigheim (BW), Hornstein
Binningen (BW), Hornstein
Birkenau (H), Unstadt
Birstein (H), Isenburg
Bödigheim (BW), Collenberg
Bodman (BW), Bodman
Boltzenburg (MV), Von Arnim
Haus Borg (NW), Kerkerinck
Braunfels (H), Solms-Braunfels
Breitenburg (SH), Rantzau
Breitenhaupt (NW), Kanne
Haus Brinke (NW), Korff-
    Bilkau
Buchholz (BW), Ow
Budingen (H), Ysenburg
Buldern (NW), Romberg
Burgsteinfurt (NW), Bentheim
Burkeim (BW), Fahnenberg
Caen (NW), Geyr
Calmsweiler (S), Buseck-Weber
Canstein (NW), Elverfeldt
Cappenberg (NW), Stein
Castell (B), Castell
Celle (NS), Lüneberg
Coesfeld (NW), Salm-Horstmar

Corvey (NW), Ratibor
Crassenstein (NW), Ansembourg
Crollage (NW), Ledebur
Dalwigksthal (H), Dalwigk
Darfeld (NW), Vischering
Derneburg (NS), Münster
Deutsch-Nienhof (SH), Hedemann-Heespen
Die Poltsdorf (B), Enderndorf
Diersburg (BW), Roeder
Diersfordt (NW), Wernigerode
Dillingen (B), Fuggers
Donaueschingen (BW), Fürstenberg
Donzdorf (BW), Rechberg
Drensteinfurt (NW), Landsberg-Velen
Dresden (SA), Wolkenstein
Bad Driburg (NW), Oeynhausen
Dulmen (NW), Croy
Durbach (BW), Windschläg
Dyck (NW), Reifferscheidt
Ebnet (BW), Gayling
Egelborg (NW), Oer
Eglofs (BW), Syrgenstein
Eichtersheim (BW), Venning
Elbenberg (H), Buttlar
Ellingen (B), Wrede
Eltville (H), Eltz
Erbach (H), Erbach
Erpernberg (NW), Wartenberg-Brenken
Erzeleben (SAA), Alvensleben
Eschenbach (B), Eschenbach
Essingen (BW), Woellwarth
Eybach (BW), Degenfeld-Schonburg
Fachsenfeld (BW), Fachsenfeld
Fischbach (B), Enderndorf

Frankenberg (B), Pöllnitz
Frankisch-Crumbach (H), Gemmingen
Furth-Burgfarrnbach (B), Pückler
Gärtringen (BW), Gärtringen
Gemünd (NW), Harff-Dreiborn
Gemünden (RP), Salis-Soglio
Gersfeld (H), Ebersberg-Froberg
Gödens (NS), Wedel
Göppingen (BW), Liebenstein
Gotha (T), Hohenlohe
Greifenberg (B), Perfall
Grevenburg (NW), Oeynhausen
Gross-Brunsrode (NS), Bülow
Grünsberg (B), Reichenbach
Guttenberg (B), Guttenberg
Burg-Guttenberg (BW), Gemmingen
Hahnstatten (RP), Bieberstein
Haidenburg (B), Aretin
Haimendorf (B), Rehlingen
Harff (NW), Mirbach
Havixbeck (NW), Twikkel
Heimerzheim (NW), Böselager
Heltorf (NW), Spee
Herbern (NW), Merveldt
Herdringen (NW), Fürstenberg
Heroldsberg (B), Geuder
Herrnstein (NW), Reichenstein
Hinnenburg (NW), Asseburg
Hohenstadt (BW), Adelmann
Höllinghofen (NW), Böselager
Hornberg (BW), Gemmingen
Hugstetten (BW), Mentzingen
Irmelshausen (B), Bibra
Jagsthausen (BW), Berlichingen
Jettingen-Eberstall (B), Stauffenberg
Kalbeck (NW), Vittinghoff

Kellenberg (NW), Hoensbroech
Kendenich (NW), Kempis
Kleinbottwar (BW), Schaubek
Königseggwald (BW),
　Aulendorf
Korschenbroich (NW),
　Wüllenweber
Kronburg (B), Westernach
Laibach (BW), Racknitz
Langenstein (BW), Douglas
Laubach (H), Solms-Laubach
Lauterbach (H), Riedesel
Lenthe (NS), Lenthe
Lich (H), Solms-Lich
Lipporg (NW), Galen
Loburg (NW), Elverfeldt
Marck (NW), Grüter
Marxwalde (BR), Hardenberg
Massenbach (BW), Massenbach
Merkstein (NW), Brauchitsch
Merlsheim (NW), Mühlen
Mespelbrunn (B), Ingelheim
Meuselwitz (SA), Seckendorff
Mitwitz (B), Würtzburg
Moyland (NW), Steengracht
Nassau (RP), Stein
Neuenburg (B), Gagern
Neuenstein (BW), Hohenlohe
Neunhof (B), Welser
Neuwied (RP), Wied
Niedenstein (BW), Venning
Niederstotzingen (BW),
　Maldegem
Oberbalzheim (BW), Balzheim
Obernzenn (B), Seckendorff
Oberstadion (BW), Schönborn
Öhringen (BW), Hohenlohe
Ostwig (NW), Lüninck
Ottingen (B), Ottingen
Pöttmes (B), Gumppenberg

Rammersdorf (B), Eyb
Ratzenried (BW), Trauchberg
Regensburg (B), Thurn-Taxis
Rentweinsdorf (B), Rotenhan
Rheda-Wiedenbrück (NW),
　Tecklenburg
Rösberg (NW), Weichs
Rötha (SA), Friesen
Rugland (B), Crailsheim
Ruhr (NW), Mühlen
Rust (BW), Böcklinsau
Schatthausen (BW),
　Ravensburg
Schillingsfürst (B), Hohenlohe
Schlatt (BW), Reischach
Schlitz (H), Görtz
Schönstein (RP), Wildenburg
Schopfheim (BW), Roggenbach
Schwarmstedt (NS), Lenthe
Schwarzenberg (B),
　Schwarzenberg
Schwarzenraben (NW), Ketteler
Schweinsberg (H),
　Schweinsberg
Sigmaringen (BW),
　Hohenzollern
Simmelsdorf (B), Simmelsdorf
Singen (BW), Enzenberg
Somborn (H), Savigny
Stapel (NW), Raitz-Frentz-
　Droste
Steisslingen (BW), Stotzingen
Stetten (BW), Stetten
Sulzfeld (BW), Ravensburg
Surenberg (NW), Heereman-
　Zuydtwyck
Syburg (B), Geyern
Tambach (B), Ortenburg
Tannhausen (BW),
　Thannhausen

Tannheim (BW), Schaesberg
Thurnau (B), Giech
Trier (RP), Kesselstatt
Trockau (B), Trockau
Ullstadt (B), Frankenstein
Volkershausen (B), Stein-
Ostheim
Vörden (NW), Haxthausen
Vornholz (NW), Nagel-
Doornick
Waake (NS), Wangenheim
Waal (B), Leyen
Wachendorf (BW), Ow-
Wachendorf
Wallerstein (B), Oettingen
Warthausen (BW), Warthausen

Weeze (NW), Loë
Weissenburg (B), Geyern
Welbergen (NW), Welbergen
Wernstein (B), Künsberg
Wertheim (BW), Löwenstein-
Wertheim
Westerholt (NW), Westerholt
Westerwinkel (NW), Merveldt
Wewer (NW), Brenken
Wiesentheid (B), Wiesentheid
Wittgenstein (NW),
Wittgenstein-Hohenstein
Wolfegg (BW), Waldburg-
Wolfegg
Worms (RP), Hernsheim
Zeil (BW), Waldburg-Zeil

Libraries (Bibliotheken)

The public libraries in cities and towns should not be neglected as a source of information. They usually contain city directories, newspapers, and local histories, all of which may date back to the middle or early part of the nineteenth century. In many places, names have been abstracted from early newspapers and placed on index cards. Many libraries also contain details of local families if they have taken an active part in the affairs of the district.

Other Records

The Church of Jesus Christ of Latter-day Saints has some miscellaneous material on microfilm from Neubrandenburg, Rostock, and Schwerin. The Landeshauptarchiv in Dresden has eighty-four volumes of parish registers from former Sachsen Garnisonsorte (military posts in Saxony).

GENEALOGICAL ASSOCIATIONS IN GERMANY

There are a number of genealogical associations in the former Federal Republic, some concerned with research and family history within the present-day political areas of "West" Germany, others concentrating on records in the "lost" territories to the east. They are all loosely associated with a national genealogical association: Deutsche Arbeitsgemeinschaft Genealogischer Verbände or D.A.G.V., Stolzingstrasse 4/13, 81927 Munich. I list the various associations below. It is important that you make contact with the one operating in your area of Germany because (a) they will probably know if someone else has already researched your family; (b) many of them have their own libraries and archives, which may contain items of vital interest to you; (c) many of them publish magazines at regular intervals and will publish small ads or queries, either free or for a small charge. Some of them only accept queries for their own members, so you might consider joining.

The D.A.G.V. issues good advice in English to people sending inquiries to them, or to the individual associations. It is worthwhile giving you a précis of the advice.

1. There is no connection between the church records of the two major denominations. If you want a search made in a church archive or register, you must know the actual religion.

2. There can be no answer to questions about an ancestor unless you know a place of origin, birth, or marriage. Inquiries based on "Germany," or "Preussen," or "near Stuttgart" cannot be answered.

3. Do all the research you possibly can in your own country through family papers, wills, obituary notices, and family Bibles.

4. If you are asking questions about several people who came from different locations, write each query on a separate sheet of paper.

5. If you have already done some research, give all the details.

6. Good English is better than bad German. Use a typewriter, or print all names of persons and places.

7. Send *four* International Reply Coupons to cover postage and expenses. Donations are appreciated.

The list I mentioned is given on the following page. It is as complete as I can make it, but bear in mind addresses can change, and there can always be additions or deletions. If you do not find one that covers your area of interest, write to the D.A.G.V. for further information.

BADEN-WÜRTTEMBERG
Verein für Familien- und Wappenkunde
Konrad-Adenauer-Strasse 8, 70173 Stuttgart
Has a good family card index.

BAYERN
Bayerischer Landsverein für Familienkunde
Winzerstrasse 68, 80797 Munich

Gesellschaft für Familienforschung in Franken
Archivstrasse 17, 90408 Nürnberg
Only concerned with the Franken (Franconia) area.

Schwäbische Forschungsmeinschaft
Universität Augsburg
Universitätstrasse 10, 86159 Augsburg

BREMEN
Gesellschaft für Familienkunde
Präsident Kennedy Platz 2, 28203 Bremen
Covers the area of Bremen and district.

HAMBURG
Genealogische Gesellschaft
Postfach 302042, 20307 Hamburg
Concerned with Hamburg, Niedersachsen, Mecklenburg, Schleswig-Holstein.

HESSEN
Hessische Familiengeschichtliche Vereinigung
Karolinenplatz 3, 64289 Darmstadt
Primary concern is the former Duchy of Hessen-Darmstadt. Very helpful to overseas inquirers if International Reply Coupons are enclosed.

Familienkundliche Gesellschaft für Nassau und Frankfurt
Niederwaldstrasse 5, 65187 Wiesbaden
Area of Nassau and Frankfurt only.

Gesellschaft für Familienkunde in Kurhessen und Waldeck
Postfach 410328, 34065 Kassel-Wilhelmshöhe.
Interested in the two districts only.

Vereingung für Familien- und Wappenkunde Fulda
Taunusstrasse 4, 36043 Fulda-Edelzell
Concerned with the Fulda area.

NIEDERSACHSEN
Familienkundliche Kommission für Niedersachsen und Bremen sowie
angrenzende ostfälische Gebiete

Schloss Ricklingen, Steinfeldstrasse 34, 30826 Garbsen 5
Concerned with Niedersachsen, Bremen, and an area of east Westfalen.

Familienkundlicher Verein Hildesheim
Wallmodenweg 2, 31141 Hildesheim
Only concerned with the Hildesheim area.

Landsverein für Familienkunde
Am Bokemohle 14-16 (Stadtarchiv), 30171 Hannover

Genealogisch-Heraldische Gesellschaft
Theaterplatz 5, Stadtarchiv, 37073 Göttingen
Only interested in this one area.

Oldenburgische Gesellschaft für Familienkunde
Lerigauweg 14, 26131 Oldenburg
Concerned with the area of the old Duchy of Oldenburg.

Ostfriesische Landschaft-Aurich
Postfach 1580, 26585 Aurich
Concerned with the Ost Friesland area and the city of Aurich.

NORDRHEIN-WESTFALEN
Westfälische Gesellschaft für Genealogie und Familienforschung
Warendorfer Strasse 25, 48145 Münster
Concerned with the old province of Westfalen.

Lippischer Heimatsbund
Bismarckstrasse 8, 32756 Detmold
The main area of interest is in the old State of Lippe.

Düsseldorfer Verein für Familienkunde
Erich Klausener Strasse 42, 40474 Düsseldorf 30

RHEINLAND-PFALZ
Arbeitsgemeinschaft für Pfälzisch-Rheinische Familienkunde
Rottstrasse 17, 67061 Ludwigshafen am Rhein

Pfalzische Geschichte und Folkskunde Bensinoring
Postfach 2860, 67657 Kaiserlautern

SAARLAND
Arbeitsgemeinschaft für Saarländische Familienkunde
Kohlweg 54, 66123 Saarbrücken
Covers only the Saarland area.

SCHLESWIG-HOLSTEIN
Schleswig-Holsteinische Gesellschaft für Familienforschung und
 Wappenkunde
Gartenstrasse 12, 24103 Kiel

Arbeitskreis für Familienforschung
Mühlentorplatz 2, 23552 Lübeck.
Only concerned with the old Free City of Lübeck.

BERLIN
Verein zur Forderung der Zentralstelle für Personen- und Familien-
geschichte
Archivstrasse 12-14, 14195 Berlin

There are also several organizations concerned with more general
areas, or with more specific subjects:

OST UND WEST PREUSSEN
Familienforschung in Ost und West Preussen
Eichstrasse 6, 25336 Elmshorn

OST DEUTSCHLAND (EAST GERMANY)
Arbeitsgemeinschaft für Ostdeutsche Familienforscher
Ernst-Moritz-Arndt Strasse 25, 53225 Bonn

MITTEL DEUTSCHLAND (CENTRAL GERMANY)
Arbeitsgemeinschaft für Mitteldeutsche Familienforschung
Emilienstrasse 1, 34121 Kassel, Hessen

Arbeitsgemeinschaft Genealogie Thüringen
Otto-Schwarzstrasse 58, 07768 Jena-Winzerla
(Branches in Erfurt, Gera, and Weimar)

WEST DEUTSCHLAND (WEST GERMANY)
Westdeutsche Gesellschaft für Familienkunde
Wallstrasse 96, 51063 Köln (Cologne)

BERLIN
Herold Verein für Heraldik
Archivstrasse 12-14, 14195 Berlin
Concerned with heraldry and noble families.

HUGENOTTEN (HUGUENOTS)
Deutscher Hugenotten-Verein
Hafenplatz 9a, 34385 Bad Karlshafen
Researches families of Huguenot descent.

There is another method of ancestor-hunting in Germany—a paid ad
in a genealogical magazine. *Familienkundliche Nachrichten* (known as
FANA) is published every two months by Verlag Degener and Co.,
Postfach 1340, 91413 Neustadt (Aisch). Send your query in English
and be short and specific; you should tell them what you know about
your German background and the approximate date of emigration of
your ancestor. They will compose the advertisement for you in German;

it will cost (at the time of this writing) about $15. The publication has a circulation of 12,000 among genealogists. You will be billed and then the query will be published. A query in this magazine can produce results. Please write and thank anyone who answers your query, and send a dollar bill to cover their postage and paper costs. The company also publishes books (in German) of genealogical interest and will mail you details on request.

There are also over 200 historical associations and societies in all the major cities and towns. It is impossible to list them all, but a letter addressed to *Historischer Verein* followed by the name of the place will probably produce results. Historical organizations very often have a great deal of information about local families even if genealogy is not the main object of their existence.

Central Office for Genealogy (Zentralstelle für Genealogie)

Although you will be looking for the same sources of information in all parts of a united Germany you will still be dealing with this organization so far as the area once known as "East Germany" is concerned. Since this is so we will be talking a great deal about this organization, and will shorten its title to Z.G. It is now part of the National Archive system of Germany and at a new location:

Zentralstelle für Genealogie
Kathe-Kollwitz-Strasse 82
04109 Leipzig

The various holdings include the following:

1. A pedigree and ancestor list which includes more than 12,000 family trees, including over two million card-indexes of individual names. If you are consulting these cards in person (and you may obtain permission to do so), you must know the system. Because of the variation in the spelling of surnames, it was decided to follow a system of phonetic spelling and file under one spelling variation only. So, for example, under the name Maier you will also find Mayer, Meier, and Meyer.

2. A catalogue of personal writings and eulogies. This covers the sixteenth to eighteenth centuries and consists of some 700 works. It is being added to on a regular basis and is certainly only in its infancy, and it includes many printed funeral orations and sermons (I have referred to this German custom earlier).

3. The Z.G. also contains photocopies and microfilms of a number of church registers of all denominations. There is no list available, but this is understandable because the additions are being made constantly and any list would soon be out of date.

4. There are more specialized items in the Z.G. records such as the following:

  (a) A list of the population of Leipzig before 1800, including the surrounding area.
  (b) Records of the Huguenots who fled from France after the bloody persecution that followed the revocation of the Edict of Nantes in 1685.

5. The library of Z.G. includes 22,000 writings on genealogical subjects, in both published and manuscript form, covering the period from the seventeenth century to the present.

6. A number of genealogists have bequeathed or surrendered their research papers to the Z.G. and these are being catalogued and indexed.

The Director of the Z.G. tells me that he and his staff are happy to help overseas inquirers. He emphasizes that requests should include as much detail as possible, particularly full names, religion, date of birth, etc., and possible location. The staff will search church records as well as their own holdings if requested. A fee will be charged and the amount quoted and paid before the search will be made. The Z.G. can be particularly useful if you are searching for information about Germans who originated in those areas now east of the Oder-Neisse frontier in Poland and the former USSR.

There are Genealogical Study Groups (Arbeitsgemeinschaften Genealogie) in all the main centers in the eastern part of Germany. The Z.G. will supply you with an up-to-date address of any genealogical group that exists in your particular area of interest.

CONTINUATION

This is usually the part of the book where the author melds together everything he has said in all previous pages and writes the magic word CONCLUSION. In a book about searching for your German roots (or any other roots) this cannot be written. Unless you are unbelievably lucky there will never be a conclusion, no end to the road, no finish to the story—there will always be gaps to be filled, questions to be answered. You may have traced your family back 500 years, but in one generation you may have a wife's first name but not her surname, in another you may have dates of baptisms and burials but no date (except an approximate one) for a marriage. These gaps will not mean your proven descent is incomplete, but they will bother you over the years, and you will keep on trying a new approach, thinking up a brilliant idea to solve the problem.

Anyway, do you really ever want to say FINISH? What would you do with your time then? If you started with your father's family, you can now try your mother's. You have grandparents to work on, and great-grandparents too. The possibilities are endless. You can even take on the mammoth project of tracing every living relative! I know one woman in New York who is doing just that—she can already produce over 300 cousins of various degrees, and she is still on the hunt for more!

Apart from the dull parade of "vital events" that make up your family tree, your search will bring you excitement and romance. You will have the thrill of the chase as, step by step, you go further back into history. You will have those magic moments when you open a long-awaited letter from Bavaria to find you have gone back another generation. You will find moments of intimacy in old letters and diaries. You may discover touching tributes to one of your ancestors—like one of my wife's

Copland forebears who had these wonderful words inscribed on the tombstone of his parents:

> If all those who well knew and could record his integrity, public spirit, and benevolence, and her amiable manners and worth, had been immortal, this memorial need not have been inscribed by their eldest son, William Copland of Colliston.
> A.D. 1808.

As you trace your family back you will want to know much more about the work they did, the clothes they wore, the houses they lived in, the area in which they were born. You can find all this in local history books, old newspapers, books on sociology, and so on. I found out many things about my sheep-farming ancestors. I know the breed they raised on the high fells above the ancestral valley of Swindale—Herdwicks; I know when they took their sheep to market in Kendal—every Wednesday; I know how much they got for their wool—8 shillings for 14 pounds in 1705; I know when they took the flocks up to the fells for the summer grazing—early in April; I know the food they ate, the clothes they wore, the furniture in their houses. These are the fascinating details that put thick foliage on the bare branches of the family tree.

During all the centuries the Baxters were raising their sheep and their children in their remote, lost dale, my wife's family—the Pearsons—were living some sixty miles away on the upper reaches of the River Tyne. Their life was very different from the Baxters'. Although they, too, had originally been hill farmers, they had developed a nose for business and were soon owning lead mines and coal mines and ever-increasing estates. They were lords of the manors of Haltwhistle and Allendale and Hexham—totaling thousands of acres of good farmland and stone quarries and rich summer grazing. They married the daughters of the Earls of Derwentwater and played an active part in the fashionable life of London and Newcastle. They sent one son to manage lead mines in Scotland and another to fight in the lost cause of the Jacobite Rebellion of 1715.

You may discover many similar stories about your ancestors if you dig deep enough. If you are lucky you may well come into possession of family treasures you do not even know about now. As you make contact with distant relatives in the old country—a cousin in the Palatinate, another one in the Black Forest—you will eventually meet, make friendships, and who knows what family heirlooms will be passed on to you?

Perhaps you will find, as I once did, the ruins of an old house once built and occupied by an ancestor. I doubt, however, if any find could be more romantic than mine. Many years ago on a spring morning, just after daybreak, I was poking about in the ruins of an old house called

Swindalehead. The silence was total, except for the sound of a few sheep grazing nearby. I found a massive beam that must have been the original support for the bedroom over the living room. Suddenly I noticed some faint carving in the wood. I rubbed away at the dirt and grime, and picked away at the indentation with an old squared nail I found. Finally I could decipher it—JB 💮 IB 1539. I knew who they were! John Baxter and his wife, Isabel Wilkinson, and 1539 was the year of their marriage. I also know that in that year John was nineteen and his wife was eighteen, and they had been given the farm as a wedding present by John's father. Standing in the ruins in the silence and the stillness of that lonely, lovely valley of my ancestors, I could picture the two youngsters setting up house together—John carving the initials in the heavy beam, and Isabel holding firm the chair on which he stood. In that moment all my ancestors crowded around me and all my searching for my roots was worthwhile.

Go forward then—there is still magic in the world, and love and warmth and happiness.

GERMAN GENEALOGICAL ASSOCIATIONS IN NORTH AMERICA

❦

The United States

American-German Historical Association
4246 South 3100 Street, Salt Lake City, UT 84117

American Historical Society of Germans from Russia
631 D Street, Lincoln, NE 68502

American Schleswig-Holstein Heritage Society
P.O. Box 313, Davenport, IA 52805

Berks County Genealogical Society
P.O. Box 14774, Reading, PA 19612

Bucks County Genealogical Society
P.O. Box 1092, Doylestown, PA 18901

Die Pommerschen Leute
1260 Westhaven Drive, Oshkosh, WI 54904

Eur-Roots Genealogy Club
377 CSW/RSSRR, Box 20, APO NY 09012

German Genealogical Index
P.O. Box 10155, Minneapolis, MN 55440

German Genealogical Society of America
2125 Wright Avenue, Suite C9, La Verne, CA 91750

German Interest Group (Chicago Genealogical Society)
c/o Ron Otto, 16828 Willow Lane Drive, Tinsley Park, IL 60477

German Research Association
P.O. Box 711600, San Diego, CA 92171

Germans from Russia Heritage Society
1008 East Central Avenue, Bismarck, ND 58501

German Texan Heritage Society
1011 Meredith Drive, P.O. Box 262, Manchaca, TX 78652

Immigrant Genealogical Society
P.O. Box 7369, Burbank, CA 91510

Krefeld Immigrants—Links Genealogy Publications
7677 Albaline Way, Sacramento, CA 95823

Lancaster Mennonite Historical Society
2215 Millstream Road, Lancaster, PA 17602

Mennonite Family History Newsletter
P.O. Box 171, Elverson, PA 19520

Mennonite Historians of Eastern Pennsylvania
565 Yoder Road, Box 82, Harleysville, PA 19438

Mid-Atlantic Germanic Society
P.O. Box 2642, Kensington, MD 20892

Orangeburg German-Swiss Genealogical Society
c/o Louis Ulmer, 3415 Pine Belt Road, Columbia, SC 29204

Palatines to America
Capital University, Box 101, Columbus, OH 43209

Genealogical Society of Pennsylvania
1300 Locust Street, Philadelphia, PA 19107

Pennsylvania German Society
P.O. Box 397, Birdsboro, PA 19508

Polish Genealogical Society
984 North Milwaukee Avenue, Chicago, IL 60622

Pommerscher Verein Freistadt
P.O. Box 204, Germantown, WI 53022

Sacramento German Genealogy Society
P.O. Box 60061, Sacramento, CA 95866

Schwenkfelder Library
1 Seminary Street, Pennsburg, PA 18073

South Central Pennsylvania Genealogical Society
P.O. Box 1824, York, PA 17405

Note: This list is as accurate as I can make it. However, I hope readers will understand that there are annual changes of officers and addresses in all voluntary associations, and there is no central registry against which the addresses given can be checked. The author will welcome assistance from readers in up-dating the information for future editions.

Canada
Kitchener Public Library (Grace Schmidt Room)
85 Queen Street North, Kitchener, Ontario N2H 2H1

Ontario German Folklore Society
c/o Mrs. M. Rowell, 131 William Street, Waterloo, Ontario N2L 1K2

Pennsylvania German Folklore Society of Ontario
c/o Mrs. R. Good, 34 Hohner Avenue, Kitchener, Ontario N2H 3G6

Waterloo-Wellington Branch, Ontario Genealogical Society
P.O. Box 66, Station Q, Toronto, Ontario M4T 2L7

Note: Germany-based genealogical organizations are listed elsewhere in this book, but should you wish to place an advertisement in a genea-logical publication asking for information about a particular ancestor, you may find it worthwhile to use *Familienkundliche Nachrichten* (see page 98).

BIBLIOGRAPHY

Note: A great many of the books listed below, both originals and re-prints, have been published by the Genealogical Publishing Company, Baltimore. The name is abbreviated to GPC, with the date of reprint as well as the original date of publication. The Bibliography is a selective one of books I have found most useful in writing this book. It does not include others written in German, or the many books written about German settlement in states other than Maryland and Pennsylvania, or Canadian provinces other than Ontario and Nova Scotia. For these you should consult your local library or genealogical society.

Baxter, A. *In Search of Your European Roots.* Baltimore, 1985, rev. ed. 1994 (GPC).

Bentz, E.M. *Decipher Germanic Records.* San Diego, 1982.

DeMarce, V. *German Military Settlers in Canada.* Reisinger, WI, 1984.

Diffenderffer, F.R. *German Immigration into Pennsylvania. . . .* 1900. Reprint, GPC, 1977.

Egle, W.H. *Early Pennsylvania Land Records.* 1893. Reprint, GPC, 1976.

Eshleman, H.F. *Historic Background and Annals of the Swiss and German Pioneer Settlers of Southeastern Pennsylvania. . . .* 1917. Reprint, GPC, 1969.

Faust, A.B. and G.M. Brumbaugh. *Lists of Swiss Emigrants in the Eighteenth Century to the American Colonies.* 2 vols. 1920–25. Reprint, GPC, 1976.

Genealogical Guide [German Ancestors from East Germany and Eastern Europe]. Neustadt (Aisch), Germany, 1984.

Glazier, I.A. and P.W. Filby. *Germans to America: Lists of Passengers Arriving at U.S. Ports 1850–1891* (in progress). Wilmington, DE, 1988–.

Hansen, M.L. *The Atlantic Migration, 1607–1860.* Cambridge, MA, 1940.

Hocker, E.W. *Genealogical Data Relating to the German Settlers of Pennsylvania and Adjacent Territory.* Baltimore, 1980 (GPC).

Irish, D.R. *Pennsylvania German Marriages.* Baltimore, 1982 (GPC).

Jones, H.Z., Jr. *The Palatine Families of New York 1710.* 2 vols. Universal City, CA, 1985 (published by the author, P.O. Box 8341, Universal City, CA 91608).

Knittle, W.A. *Early Eighteenth Century Palatine Emigration.* 1937. Reprint, GPC, 1965.

MacWethy, L.D. *The Book of Names Especially Relating to the Early Palatines and the First Settlers in the Mohawk Valley.* 1933. Reprint, GPC, 1969.

Meynen, E. *Bibliography on the Colonial Germans of North America* (originally published as *Bibliography on German Settlements in Colonial North America).* Leipzig, Germany, 1937. Reprint, GPC, 1982.

Moltman, G. *Germans to America 1683–1983,* Stuttgart, Germany, 1982.

Nead, D.W. *The Pennsylvania-German in the Settlement of Maryland.* 1914. Reprint, GPC, 1975.

Newman, H.W. *The Flowering of the Maryland Palatinate.* 1961. Reprint, GPC, 1984.

Pennsylvania German Society. *Pennsylvania German Church Records.* 3 vols. Baltimore, 1983 (GPC).

_____. *Pennsylvania German Fraktur.* Breinigsville, PA, 1983. Examples of German script.

Rupp, I.D. *A Collection of Upwards of Thirty Thousand Names of German . . . Immigrants in Pennsylvania from 1727 to 1776.* 1876. Reprint, GPC, 1965.

Schenk, T., R. Froelke, and I. Bork. *The Wuerttemberg Emigration Index.* 5 vols. (total 8 vols. projected). Salt Lake City, 1986–.

Simmendinger, U. *True and Authentic Register of Persons . . . Who in the Year 1709 . . . Journeyed from Germany to America.* 1934. Reprint, GPC, 1966.

Smith, C. and A. *Encyclopedia of German-American Genealogical Research.* New York, 1976.

Staudt, R.W. *Palatine Church Visitations, 1609, Deanery of Kusel.* 1930. Reprint, GPC, 1980.

Steigerwald, J. *Tracing Romania's German Minority* (Danubian Swabians). Winona, MN, 1985.

Stoever, J.C. *Early Lutheran Baptisms and Marriages in Southeastern Pennsylvania* (originally published as *Records of Rev. John Casper Stoever*). 1896. Reprint, GPC, 1982.

Strassburger, R.B. and W.J. Hinke. *Pennsylvania German Pioneers: A Publication of the Original Lists of Arrivals in the Port of Philadelphia from 1727 to 1808*. 3 vols. 1934. Reprint, GPC, 1966.

Tepper, M. *American Passenger Arrival Records: A Guide to the Records of Immigrants Arriving at American Ports by Sail and Steam*. Second Edition. Baltimore, 1993. (GPC).

_____. *Emigrants to Pennsylvania, 1641–1819 . . . from the Pennsylvania Magazine of History and Biography*. Baltimore, 1975 (GPC).

_____. *Passenger Arrivals at the Port of Baltimore, 1820–1834*. Baltimore, 1982 (GPC).

_____. *Passenger Arrivals at the Port of Philadelphia, 1800–1819*. Baltimore, 1986 (GPC).

Wolfert, M. *List of Passengers from Bremen to New York (1868–1871)*. Baltimore, 1993 (GPC).

Yoder, D. *Pennsylvania German Immigrants, 1709–1786*. Baltimore, 1980 (GPC).

_____. *Rhineland Emigrants*. Baltimore, 1981 (GPC).

Zimmerman, G.J. and M. Wolfert. *German Immigrants: Lists of Passengers from Bremen to New York (1847–1867)*. Baltimore, 1985–88 (GPC).

Canada

Baxter, A. *In Search of Your Roots*. Toronto, 1978, 1991.

_____. *In Search of Your Canadian Roots*. Baltimore, 1989, rev. ed. 1994 (GPC).

Bell, W.P. *The Foreign Protestants and the Settlement of Nova Scotia*. Toronto, 1961.

DesBrisay, M.B. *History of Lunenburg County*. Halifax, 1870.

Eby, E. *A Biographical History of Early Settlers and Their Descendants in Waterloo Township*. Kitchener, 1895. Reprint, 1971.

Fretz, J.W. *People Apart*. St. Jacobs, 1971.

Johnson, R. *150 Years First Mennonite Church* [Kitchener]. Kitchener, 1963.

Leibbrandt, G. *Little Paradise* [Waterloo County, 1800–1937]. Kitchener, 1980.

Moyer, W.G. *This Unique Heritage* [Waterloo County]. Kitchener, 1971.

Punch, T. *Genealogical Research in Nova Scotia*. Halifax, 1978.
Reaman, G.E. *The Trail of the Black Walnut* [Pennsylvania to Canada]. Toronto, 1965.
Uttley, W.V. *A History of Kitchener* [1865–1944]. Kitchener, 1937. Reprint, 1975.

Note: Three early German newspapers (*Canada Museum, Deutsche Canadier,* and *Berliner Journal*) have been indexed for birth, marriage, and death entries by the Kitchener Public Library. Two ethnic German societies, which can be reached through the library, are the Ontario German Folklore Society and the Pennsylvania German Folklore Society of Ontario.

INDEX